The Murder of Dawn Magyar

Pete Dover

Published by Trellis Publishing, 2021.

While every precaution has been taken in the preparation of this book, the publisher assumes no responsibility for errors or omissions, or for damages resulting from the use of the information contained herein.

THE MURDER OF DAWN MAGYAR

First edition. July 1, 2021.

Copyright © 2021 Pete Dover.

ISBN: 979-8224178377

Written by Pete Dover.

THE MURDER OF DAWN MAGYAR
& OTHER STORIES

PETE DOVER

The Longest Search – 30 Years 'Til Justice

Sometimes, we can have it all, then see everything that is important to us whisked away in a second. That must be how things felt to Don Magyar when his wife failed to return home from a simple shopping trip one cold, foggy Saturday in January 1973.

Carly Simon was on top of the billboard charts with 'You're So Vain'; Stevie Wonder was about to take her place. Soon Roberta Flack would head the best sellers with 'Killing Me Softly With His Song.' That was the time; gentle, hopeful. Ryan O Neal was starring with his young daughter, Tatum, in 'Paper Moon.' The world of the Magyars was an idealistic and peaceful place, at least on the surface.

In Washington, the scandal of Watergate was growing and Nixon was pulling every string he could – and a few he couldn't – to try to stay in office; but that was all a million miles away from rural Michigan.

Don and Dawn were the perfect couple for the time. Optimistic, honest, and young with the world at their feet. They had been childhood sweethearts and dated throughout high school. It was a known fact that Don and Dawn were a couple now and would always be a couple. That was the way it was. They had a young son, just one year old when that hopeful world would be shattered.

It was just another ordinary Saturday and Dawn Magyar was gone. She had never met her assailant. All that she did was choose to do some food shopping for the family at a supermarket where, by chance, Jerald Wingeart chose to drive to that afternoon.

Dawn was born in Corunna, Michigan in March of 1952. She had a happy and safe childhood. She met Don, and that happy, secure life continued. They moved to the small village of Chesaning, Michigan, her son was born and she committed to bringing him up. Money was tight, but the couple could not have been happier.

Snow lay on the ground, turning to ice in the bitter Michigan winter that Saturday, and Dawn borrowed a pick-up truck from a friend to make the twenty-five minute journey south to the small town of Owosso, which was just about big enough to host a supermarket or two.

She completed her shopping; we know that because the groceries she bought were later discovered untouched in the car. She must have just finished loading them when Wingeart approached. He always denied the crime, and has refused to discuss how it happened. While CCTV was around back then, it wasn't in places like Owosso. Again, a small quiet town where bad things simply didn't happen.

But police would later find her keys discarded on the floor of the barren car park where she had left the borrowed pick up. There were no signs of a struggle, no reports from other shoppers of some kind of disturbance in the parking lot. Who can imagine the shock and fear that traveled through the young woman when the stranger approached? Did he threaten her with a gun? Did he just grab her? Somehow, he got Dawn to his car and drove her north and across the border line to Saginaw County.

In the supermarket, Dawn had bumped into an old acquaintance. Purely by chance, she joined the queue at the checkout behind Janice Simpson, a friend whom she had not seen for a while. They had chatted about babies and husbands and the price of milk, as people do. Then Janice had packed her bags and left Dawn to put her own goods through the checkout. That was the last she ever saw of her casual friend.

'I came into the check-out lane and I noticed a good friend of mine, Dawn Magyar' recalled Janice, explaining the chance encounter.

She was horrified when the news broke that she was the last person to hold a friendly conversation with Dawn.

'It just really bothered me inside to know that she had gone,' said Janice later.

It bothered the police as well. Leads were suggested, but detectives always ended up staring at a blank wall with no clues. People were interviewed, but they had nothing to say. It was as though a young woman with a happy family and everything ahead of her had simply vanished.

The local press were very interested in the story. Events like this did not happen in Ossowa and its region.

'Truth is stranger than fiction. You couldn't have made this up,' said Helen Bough, the managing editor at Argus Press, the town's newspaper.

The Michigan police department placed Detective Bart Barnes in charge of the investigation. He began his work by looking at the possibilities surrounding Dawn's disappearance. It quickly became clear that foul play had taken place.

Detective Barnes told the makers of 'The Investigators', a TV documentary about the case made after Wingeart was finally caught: 'She had no problems whatsoever, the marriage was on solid ground.'

'It did not enter my mind...that she left of her own accord.' Barnes continued. 'Here was this sweet young woman, the mother of a small child, and she just disappeared.' As the investigation began to dry up, police turned to the public for support. The local sheriff asked for help to search for the missing woman. He was overwhelmed by the response. A crowd gathered at the local court house. Around 4000 volunteers had turned up to assist with the search.

They spread out to the East and the West to begin with, covering about 15 miles in their search, then they headed north to the county line. Nothing was found, and once more the police had no idea where to turn next.

But Dawn's brother was clear that there would be no good news coming about his sibling. 'Knowing my sister as I do,' Dawn's brother said. 'She was not going anywhere, she was not going to hide.' He was certain that she had been the victim of foul play.

A month of frustrating and fruitless activity followed. Then, on March 4th 1973, six weeks after Dawn's disappearance, the police were given some information which revived their investigation. Two boys were out in the quiet countryside of Saginaw County. Eleven-year old Wayne Somers and his older brother Bill were in the woods near their farm. They were checking sap levels of trees. Wayne headed down a trail when he saw something light blue clothing in the distance. 'I could see the jacket and the legs of a woman lying on the ground,' he recalled later.

Wayne ran to get his older brother. Bill circled the body, which was lying spread out on its front. Having his brother there also gave Wayne additional confidence. He too went close to the body. They realized that the woman lying before them was dead. The icy cold weather had helped to preserve her body, and the face they saw rang a bell in their minds. They recalled the news of the disappearance of a young woman some weeks earlier, in the next county just to the south. They guessed it was Dawn.

'She had been walked into the woods,' Bart Barnes said. 'They were no drag marks. Her right arm was curled behind her back where somebody had had hold of her.' Although she was clothed, investigators later found that her under garments were missing. The autopsy report stated that she had 'a bullet removed from her head.' It was 'goldtone' ammunition, the sort used in a .22 weapon. In fact, she had been shot once in the back and twice in the head.

The body was less than a mile across the county line, just a short distance from where the search had stopped. But the location in which Dawn was found offered another small clue to the police. The road to the Somers' farm was long, dark and lonely. It was not the sort of location generally known unless somebody had particular knowledge of the area. 'It would seem nearly impossible to arrive there after dark unless you knew in advance that you were coming' said Wayne Somers. 'It had to be someone from this area.'

Somers was wrong, but just by a little bit...

The community of Owosso was the sort of gentle, backwater town we imagine from the 1970s. Just seventy-thousand inhabitants lived there in the early part of that decade. It was the kind of place where you did not lock the door to your house or car, the sort of place where things like the murder of Dawn Magyar just did not happen.

'It was a shock, created an underlying fear factor,' Tony Hornus, editor of the Argus Press said.

He had gone to school with both Dawn and Don. He recalled Dawn as a sweet and kind girl, but not really remarkable in any way. The girl next door.

'She was just a sweet girl,' he recalled. 'Very personable, very kind'.

She was an able student, and she and Don had been together throughout High School. In fact, neither dated anybody else.

Suspicion soon fell on the people closest to the victim. But in this case, these suspicions were quickly allayed. Police carried out a thorough investigation, although Bart Barnes had little doubt from early on that the killer of Dawn was somebody from outside her tight knit group. Indeed, although he spoke with Don, he soon eliminated him from further interrogation. Officers investigated Don's whereabouts, but he was simply babysitting their son while Dawn went out shopping.

Forensic science was a very young subject in those days, but police carried out blood grouping and blood type tests, comparing their samples with evidence found on Dawn's body.

They had some evidence, but not a lot.

'We had blood type from the suspect,' Barnes said. 'We had the fact that she had been shot with two Remington peters .22 long-rifle shell, and one Winchester long rifle shell.'

The public deluged the police with calls. Suspects were suggested. A member of the public reported a man who was known to have had a crush on Dawn. Another told of a man living nearby with marital problems. But nothing led them any further. The press kept the story going. Elaine Bough covered the story completely as editor of the local paper. 'This was one of our own, this was personal,' she said later. 'It wasn't just another story.'

It was June of 1974 before police got their first big break in the case. Some boys had been fishing and swimming in the local Shiawassee River, and they had played at floating over the edge of the dam. One reached down as he was climbing back up the small drop. He had stepped on something that felt different to the normal stones and mud; it was the pistol that had fired one of the shots which killed Dawn.

But the river had damaged the gun. The crime lab was unable to do anything with it. The gun was just too rusty. However, Barnes guessed that this weapon might, one day, provide the key to solving the murder. After the crime lab had tried, and failed, to find clues on it, he kept working with the weapon himself. Eventually Barnes managed to the get the chamber of the weapon open. In it he discovered three unused shells, and three cartridges which had already been fired. These matched the shells discovered in Dawn's body. Without doubt, he knew that they now had the murder weapon. Matters were beginning to come together. But back then, Bart Barnes had no idea how long it would take for them to be resolved.

Despite the rust, the serial number was still visible on the gun. They put out a trace in an attempt to find its owner.

Eventually, it was discovered to have been manufactured in Germany. From there it had been shipped to California, and on to a pawn shop in Yuma, Arizona. The police there discovered the owner of the Pawn shop had now moved to Panama City in Florida. Astonishingly, on interviewing the former shopkeeper, they discovered that he had retained all of his records.

The man traced back through his papers and found that he had sold the gun back in 1965 to somebody called Robert Shaw. Unsurprisingly, given the time that had passed, Robert Shaw was no longer at the home where he lived when he bought the gun. Nevertheless, police retained the hope that he might still be in the city of Yuma. Back then, the kinds of databases which will throw up an address in seconds were nothing but an unlikely dream, so the police resorted to more mundane methods of seeking their man. They looked through the phone book. Yet the name Robert Shaw was a common one, and police identified several people with that title. They spoke to them all, but none knew anything about the gun. Another dead end.

Still, discoveries, if infrequent, kept happening. Another group of boys were playing in the river, and they found something important. By now, it was the summer of 1976, more than three years after Dawn's murder. They were swimming on the opposite side to where the gun had been discovered, splashing around in the north bank of the river. It was here that the boys discovered her wallet.

Now police were able to put together a probable picture of her last movements. She had been abducted in the supermarket car park. From there, she had been taken north into the next county, where the poor woman was raped and shot, her body left in the open. The killer had then headed back to Owosso, and there he had dumped the gun in one side of the river and his victim's wallet in the other. Clearly, he hoped that the two were too far apart to be found and linked, if indeed they were ever discovered.

After that sudden burst of good news for the investigation, more progress stalled. Detective Barnes, though, was determined to continue his search for the killer. But his efforts proved to be in vain. In 1979, with no more success in his mission, he retired from the Michigan State Police. 'It always bothered me,' he said, 'there were other unsolved murders but this one, a young mother, it just bothered me a lot more.'

The case stayed with Helene Bough as well. 'Everything went back to normal, yes we were not as afraid anymore, but nobody forgot.'

Without Bart Barnes to keep the investigation fresh it went cold. Nothing more happened for fifteen years. But by the early 1990s the use of DNA evidence was beginning to emerge, although it was still a young science; indeed many courts in the US refused to accept it in their cases. However, in Michigan police were embracing this aid to their work. It was a new tool to help in their investigations. And any assistance the overworked department could get was something they were happy to receive.

In 1994, Gail Tobin was a Michigan State detective. She was given a series of cold case files which might, with the advances in DNA evidence taking place, now be solvable. One of those cases was the murder of Dawn Magyar. 'There was evidence,' she said, 'taken from Dawn Magyar's body which I believed would lend itself to DNA testing.'

She was also aware that, back in the 1970s, Bart Barnes and his colleagues had identified a list of suspects. Their problem was that they lacked the technical evidence to either dismiss these suspects from their inquiries or to launch a case against them. But semen had been removed from Dawn's body, findings kept in the hope that one day technology would be advanced enough to make some use from the samples. This showed astonishing foresight from Bart Barnes and perhaps reflected his determination to see the case solved, even if it was not something that would happen during his professional life. Now, it seemed, the day when his planning would bear results had arrived.

No less than ninety-eight separate packages of evidence had been retrieved when Dawn's body was found, and most of those would prove useful as Tobin employed DNA science on the samples.

Now they had the evidence which allowed them to revisit that original list of suspects. Who knows what panic and concern hit those men when they received a knock at the door, or an unexpected phone call about a matter now long past, but the DNA evidence served to eliminate them one by one.

Ann Chamberlain was the forensics specialist who tested the samples. Yet the process was still slow. In 1998, with not much further progress achieved, Tobin was transferred to another department, and was replaced by another investigator, Marc Pendergraft. The murder inquiry into the death of Dawn was the first he would lead. 'It's the mistakes that the criminal makes that solves the crime,' he explained 'the clues he leaves behind.'

Pendergraft revisited the relevant crime scenes. He was able to eliminate the final two suspects on the original list, thanks to the ongoing improvement in DNA technology. But as for progress in identifying a killer; there was none. Dawn was the all-American girl; nobody had a bad word for her, her life was virtuous and there were no skeletons in her cupboards which could lead detectives towards a new suspect.

To Detective Pendergraft, the solution to this crime appeared to be in the gun. It had somehow made its way across virtually the entire country, from Arizona to Michigan. He felt that if he could find the mysterious Robert Shaw, the weapon's owner, then the chances of finding a solution to the crime would increase significantly.

Of course, the police's storage of and access to information had moved on substantially since Bart Barnes had scoured the pages of a telephone book, using it to find the numbers of local Robert Shaws. Now police had a data base of driving licenses which covered the entire country.

They entered the name into the data base, and were able to reduce the number of finds by inserting an approximate age – they knew the man had been at least 18 when he originally purchased the gun back in 1965. Twenty nine possibilities were thrown up by the computer.

Amazingly, one of these Robert Shaws turned out to be the man they were seeking. He was a truck driver who lived less than an hour from the town where Dawn had been murdered. To locate the man, discover he was still alive and be able to speak with him looked like the most outside of bets, but it had returned Pendergraft's investment of time fifty fold.

While Shaw was clear about purchasing the gun, he could not remember what had happened to it. Alarm bells began to sound in the minds of the investigators. The new suspect was taken in for questioning, blood was taken and he was given a polygraph test. It soon became clear that he was not the killer, but detectives were certain that he might know more about the gun than he was telling them.

Finally, after hours of questioning, something triggered a flashback in Shaw's mind. Jerald Wingeart. The man who had destroyed Shaw's marriage, running away with his wife, leaving him alone.

Shaw recalled that his ex-wife had told him that Wingeart had been accused of rape, and Shaw could not understand why, in those circumstances, his ex-wife would want to partner up with the man. But she believed that he had been tried and exonerated. However, when police investigated more deeply, they discovered that Wingeart was far from innocent. He had spent years in prison back in the 1960s – for rape. He had also been a key suspect in a subsequent murder investigation, but had avoided a guilty verdict when the case against him was dropped due to a technicality relating to the police's gathering of evidence.

Now it seemed as though time had turned the man into a respected member of his community. Prendergraft recalls: 'People saw him basically as a good person, someone who was friendly. A very intelligent person, an expert on computers.' In fact, Wingeart had been one of the computer technicians behind the Michigan State lottery.

At the time the police had him in their sights, he was married to his fourth wife and working at Daimler Chrysler, operating in their payroll department. He had moved to Detroit. Investigations showed that, at school, Wingeart had been something of a role model. Tall, athletic, and intelligent. Like Don Magyar, he too had married his childhood love. But then, in 1960, tragedy had hit his life. His young son had died, and a year later that first wife filed for divorce.

It was just days after this that he committed his first rape. Now, forty years on police were sure that their suspect would not cooperate if they sought any kind of DNA sample from him. Instead, they set up surveillance and waited for him to leave something behind from which they could extract the DNA they required. Their target kindly obliged, leaving some cigarette butts that contained his DNA.

The match between the DNA on the cigarette butts and that taken from a vaginal swab from Dawn Magyar displayed a close match. In fact, the chances of such a match occurring by accident were nearly 16 quad-million to one. In other words, there was no reasonable possibility that the findings were anything other than a proper match.

While the DNA evidence was conclusive, by itself that was unlikely to be enough to put a killer from 30 years previously behind bars. More evidence was needed. The police were in luck. Police knew that, back in 1973, Wingeart had been in the Owosso area. He was visiting a friend. He could now be placed at the location of the crime. More information began to surface as investigations deepened. It became apparent that Wingeart was a man who liked going on long drives; he enjoyed grabbing a beer and drifting through the back roads. Prendergraft believes that this was not just for the pleasure of driving or viewing the countryside. He believes that the killer would take these opportunities for finding victims and searching out safe places to dump the bodies that followed.

This predilection for searching out the quiet and unused roads of the areas he explored suggested that Wayne Somers' thoughts, stated earlier, had some validity. Wingeart might not be local, knowing the farm where the victim was found, but he could well have stumbled across it on one of his jaunts.

Eventually, police took the decision to interview their man. He denied all knowledge of Dawn, and accused the police of harassing him. He refused to answer questions without an attorney present. But police believed that they had enough. They knew that, through his relationship with Shaw's wife, he had the opportunity to steal the gun, they knew that he was in the area during the time in question. They had the DNA evidence. Prosecutors agreed that the case could go ahead, and Wingeart was arrested and placed on trial. This took place in November 2001.

The Shiawassee County Prosecutor at the time of the trial, Randy O. Colbry, knew that matters would not be cut and dried. 'In a jury trial, there is no such thing as a slam dunk,' he said at the time.

By now, close to thirty years after the crime, Wingeart was no longer the athletic man he had been in his youth. He was getting on in years, respectable looking with neat, grey hair. The muscle of his youth had turned steadily to flab, and he was slightly portly. For all the world, he appeared like a kindly grandfather. To believe that a man such as this could have raped and murdered a young woman was something about which the jury would need seriously convincing.

But despite the time that had elapsed between the crime and the trial, the prosecution team had one element of luck on their side. Everybody involved at the time of Dawn's murder was still alive, and able to testify. Even Wayne Somers, now a grown man rather than the innocent looking boy with the slightly too long hair he had been back in 1973, was able to offer his evidence at the trial.

Nevertheless persuading a jury was still tricky. The prosecution's strongest weapon was the DNA evidence linking Wingeart to the crime. Vince Green, the accused man's lawyer, chose not to dispute this, but instead argued that the sex between the two had been consensual. Green argued that expert testimony proved that this liaison could have happened many days before the murder, not just on the day of it. But Ann Chamberlain's findings challenged such a view. Her analysis of the sperm sample indicated that it was fresh; whoever had sex with the attractive young woman was also, it would seem, responsible for her death.

After two weeks of testimony the case was given to the jury; two days of deliberation followed and the verdict was returned. 'Guilty'. Wingeart visibly shuddered as the announcement was made, and his head dropped forward. He was sentenced to life in prison without the possibility of parole.

At the end of the day, the chances of this loyal, loving mother and wife choosing to have consensual sex with a stranger were just too remote for the jury to give credence to them.

It seems as though Dawn Magyar lost her life in violent, horrific circumstances purely by chance. If ever there was a case of being in the wrong place at the wrong time, this was it. The best explanation police have as to why she became Wingeart's victim is that she was there. He just happened to drive into the car park as she was leaving the store. That was enough.

'She was a good student, she was a faithful wife, she was a good mother,' Barnes recalled.

'She was just an all-round good person.'

THEY KILLED MOM

15

PETE DOVER

CHRISTINE GOODMAN

Nicole Kasinskas was a quiet, unassuming teenage girl. She was born and raised in Nashua, New Hampshire to Anthony Kasinskas and Jeanne Domenico.

"I lived with both of my parents and my younger brother until I was eleven years old," Nicole said. "And my parents divorced and my Dad moved out."

"I think after my parents got divorced and I was dealing with that, I became a little bit angrier. I had a little bit more resentment towards him, and it did change my perspectives about myself and about life in general, I guess even as an eleven year old."

In May of 2002, she found "romance" as a fifteen year old on-line with eighteen-year old Billy Sullivan.

Sullivan lived in a town called Willmantic where he worked as a line cook at McDonald's.

"Nicole hadn't had a lot of boyfriends," prosecuting attorney Kirsten Wilson said . "She was really caught up by the attention by this guy who was saying amazing things to her about how beautiful she was and what she meant to him."

They would communicate daily through e-mail, letters and phone calls. Despite not having met in person, they both declared love for each other within days, speaking of marriage and planning their future together.

"They filled in sort of the gaps of everyday communication and relationships with fantasies and making these assumptions on who the other person was," Wilson said.

"He lived in Connecticut and so our relationship was almost one hundred percent over the phone," Nicole said. "But it became everything to me very quickly because of the amount of attention that he paid me, and I didn't really feel that I was getting that from anywhere else."

Nicole had been vulnerable to Sullivan's Internet advances as she was a loner with very few friends in high school. She was routinely bullied at school by other girls. On one occasion, she was walking down the hall and one of her bullies had pulled her sweatpants down to her ankles. Nicole was not wearing any underwear, furthering the humiliation. Nicole refused to go back to school the next day after that incident.

"The bullying at school certainly made Nicole vulnerable to someone like Sullivan," forensic psychologist Fiona Russo said. "She's lonely, she's being picked on at school and completely humiliated. She stuck to herself and so when some guy pays attention to her, even when it is only online, her fantasy life goes into overdrive. She's able to project things on him that he doesn't deserve or merit."

The more severe the bullying became, the more Nicole began to withdraw and cling to Sullivan.

"As I got older, it was easier for me to isolate from people," Nicole said. "I think at that point I had just gotten used to being more alone as opposed to being around people. And it just became a part of who I was. Maybe if I was more open or maybe if someone had tried harder to reach out, that it could've been different."

Nicole's mom, Jeanne, was her best friend. Jeanne worked at an elementary school for a period of time, holding down such jobs as a crossing guard, a lunchroom monitor, and a paraprofessional for about three years before taking a job where she worked on group contracts for the Benefits, Brokers and Administration department.

"Jeanne Domenico was well loved in the community," Wilson said. "Hard worker. Really sort of a bright, energetic, sweet woman. She was trying to make her daughter happy."

Despite the bullying at school, Nicole got straight A's at school and made her mother happy whenever she made the honor roll.

"School really became my self-worth and I really identified with, like whatever my grades were," Nicole said. "However I was doing in school I felt it reflected on me personally, because I felt that it was so much a part of who I was. I never got in trouble in middle school. I never got spoken to. I never had a detention. It never really crossed my mind to do anything that would be against the rules."

"It would have been helpful if there was more of an acknowledgment that I was doing so well. I think it also would've been helpful if there was more involvement with guidance or something. Just more of a like a check-in...see how things are going."

"Somehow, someway, Nicole got lost in the cracks," Russo said. "That in no way justifies what she did. It may be how she justified it during this time. Her parents are divorced. She doesn't see her Dad. Her mom is working all the time. There had to have been days where she felt intense loneliness Going to school just to be ignored or bullied. To a fourteen year old girl you really may not see the light at the end of the tunnel. So you seek an outlet. Some turn to drugs. Nicole found her own drug in the form of the words that came out of Sullivan's keyboard."

MOTHER AND DAUGHTER TROUBLES

At least on the surface, there were no problems between mother and daughter.

Until Nicole ventured on-line and met Billy Sullivan.

Her mother found out about the relationship and wanting to make her daughter happy, drove the young teenager out to Connecticut so she could meet Sullivan for the first time.

"This was a two hour drive from Nashua to the place in Connecticut where Sullivan lived," Russo said. "It is easy to say here is where Jeanne made a fatal mistake. But in her mind, it is all innocent. Her daughter is fourteen and begging her to drive out to meet this guy. Begging and begging. Until she finally she relents."

More visits followed but friends and classmates knew little of the teen's relationship. Sullivan had informed some of his friends that he had a girlfriend that was "out of state." Other than that, he revealed very little about his personal life.

"He's quiet, he didn't really like to talk," recalled Danny Goss who was a classmate of Sullivan. "But he was good in school and didn't get in any trouble."

"I think the relationship intensified to a degree that Jeanne herself didn't anticipate," Russo said. "And it is easy to play Monday morning quarterback here but there had to have been some kind of father figure present to say 'hey, this is an eighteen-year old working at McDonald's. You are a fourteen year old honor student. You have a future. Don't blow it on this guy. But it isn't like teens listen to you anyway."

The two teenagers soon discussed the prospect of moving in together. Her mother quickly objected to this idea as well as nixing the idea of Nicole sharing a joint bank account with Sullivan.

But the young man later stayed overnight one weekend with Nicole's mother's full consent.

The relationship is the first for Nicole. She pedestalizes Sullivan as everything she has fantasized about is coming true.

"Nicole had a void in her life," Russo said. "When her parents divorced it certainly affected her psychologically in the way she viewed men. Then along comes Sullivan whose older and more experienced. She gets the love from him that perhaps she sought from her father. The older man, wiser than his years, showering her with attention. She was vulnerable to that."

"Her father didn't have too much to do with her after the divorce. She had that longing in her heart for that male figure. And along came Sullivan."

PERSONAL DEMONS OF HIS OWN

Sullivan, however, had his own personal demons he was fighting.

"He did have mental health issues," Wilson said. "He had been hospitalized a number of times. During high school he had some behavioral issues. Some anxiety, that kind of thing."

It was later revealed that Sullivan had been on numerous psychiatric medications to curb his depression, anger and schizophrenia. He had been weaning himself off the meds, however, and on one occasion he engaged in an argument with Nicole's mother over dinner.

Jeanne had asked Billy if she liked the dinner she had prepared. He said yes and then Jean made the comment that "I bet you don't get that too much at home."

Sullivan was highly defensive over anything that involved his home life. When Jeanne made that comment, he turned hostile.

"Sullivan was protective of his home life," Russo said. "If anyone insulted his mother or if he even perceives that someone is insulting his mother then he gets abusive. He did this to Jeanne, who had obviously made nothing more than an idle comment. That was the first warning sign and the relationship should have ended then and there."

Nicole, however, defended her young beau and from that moment the tug of war for her heart began.

"Nicole's own naivete comes to bore at this point," Russo said. "She has no experience with boys and here is this older guy that she looks up to, almost as a father figure of sorts, who turns her against her own family. Against the one person who loved her the most. Her mother. It is a tug of war that the mother loses simply because her daughter's hormones are raging and she doesn't yet have the emotional capacity to know any better."

After a year of dating, in August of 2003, Sullivan drove out to Nashua to spend a week with Nicole. By this time, they are both fed up with Nicole's mother's objections to their ideas of cohabitation.

"Our relationship was definitely emotionally abusive," Nicole said. "And I think now over time, from looking at it, my perspectives on that have changed so much. I feel like he is responsible for his actions and I am responsible for mine. I didn't really get that and I feel like in order to be emotionally abused, in order to stand for it and stay in it, there's gotta be something missing in you. There's gotta be something hurting already, something is not there, something's not right. And that needs to be figured out, found and fixed. Regardless of how a child is acting or what's coming off,there's more inside that kids need help with or guidance or just to have some type of connection with someone. You need to have relationships with people ahead of time, so that when the bad stuff does happen does happen you don't just come in to it expecting to work it out. Like, you need to have firm foundation with that person in order to work it out."

Nicole continued to side with Sullivan against her mother. The two argued constantly, Sullivan's influence quickly become apparent in Nicole's attitude toward her mother as she found fault with everything she did.

The two teens began discussing an unheard of option.

They began discussing the prospect of killing her mother.

"Well, this is where it starts getting...it's a scary business for me," Nicole said in a jailhouse interview. "I'll tell you that. I feel like I"m gonna cry. I don't talk about this stuff so this is really the first time. I think that my relationship with my mom was good. It was fine. I loved my mom. And...that changed. When...I'm not saying I stopped loving my mom, but...our relationship changed. I'm not gonna say that we were the most open because we weren't. We didn't talk about every little thing. I don't remember ever once talking about my parents' divorce with either of them. But the thing is, we didn't really talk about much of anything. When I was fourteen, I became involved with seventeen year old boy. This is really stemming into why I'm here (in jail) now."

OUT OF CONTROL

"Emotions begin to run high as Sullivan ups the ante in his hatred for Nicole's mother," Russo said. "Nicole is emotionally underdeveloped and has to choose between her mother and her 'man.' It is easy to look at it hindsight but with the teenaged girl's warp logic, she sees Sullivan as her entire world now. So she will do anything for him. Even murder."

Nicole's mom really didn't realize the danger that Sullivan was. She began doing what every mom does, demanding that her daughter stop seeing him, stop chatting with him and concentrate on her schoolwork. Nicole, on the other hand, remained fervent in her desire to move to Connecticut to move in with Sullivan.

"Jeanie, rightfully so, said 'you're fifteen you're finishing school,'" Wilson said. "'You're not moving to Connecticut' and that really upset both Nicole and Billy."

The prospect of not seeing Nicole had an adverse emotional effect on Billy.

"He started talking about killing himself…on the road…driving into a big truck because of leaving me..because of his sadness over it," Nicole recalled. "And I think now it just sounds silly, you know? But it wasn't then, and it was terrifying to me because I didn't…I didn't know how to…because of the way that our relationship was. Because he had become so much a part of my life. I mean, I really didn't feel like I was anything without him. I had nothing in my life at that time…I felt…at that time. So the thought of losing him in that way just wasn't okay with me. And that is unfortunately when conversations started about ultimately what happened. I guess I really I don't really go into too many details but I was sixteen and he was eighteen at that time. And I guess I should give you some background. He killed my mom and I was a part of it. I was not physically there but I knew and I helped him. I was, you know, going through the motions of what was being done. But mentally and emotionally, I don't think I was fully there. I don't think I was fully getting it."

"It was emotional manipulation," Russo said. "It is all so scary romantic for a fifteen year old girl to have some guy who is so in love with her that he is going to kill himself because he can't be with her. She has no one in her life to say 'this guy is a loser nutcase.' There isn't anyone that can talk sense to her. So she falls for the emotional manipulation of a highly disturbed but cunning con man."

Billy had convinced the depressed Nicole that her mother was an obstacle to both hers and his happiness.

"I really just did whatever I could to maintain that relationship because I didn't want to lose that," Nicole said. "I didn't want to lose him. And I quickly learned how it would go if I didn't always do everything that he wanted me to do. At that point...you know, getting to be fifteen...sixteen years old...I would fight more with my mom and there was a lot more to fight about, especially with, you know, this relationship that I was having with this kid."

THE FINAL PLAN

The couple tried different methods to murder Jeanne Domenico.

First they tried to poison Jeanne's coffee. The teens had placed Dimetapp, Benadryl and other drugs into Jeanne's coffee creamer in the refrigerator.

Jeanne used the creamer but didn't die and evidently remained ignorant of the plot on her life. The teens then added bleach to the creamer, wanting to strengthen the amount of poison. It was unclear in a court affidavit if Jeanne ever drank from the spiked creamer again.

The next idea was to set Nicole's mattress on fire with a candle. That idea didn't work because the bedding was made of fire retardant material.

It is unclear how the teens planned to fire up the mattress, whether they sneaked into her Nicole's bedroom and tried to fire up the mattress while she slept.

The third idea was to blow up the fuel oil tank in Jeanne's house. The teens had tied two ropes together which would serve as a wick. Their idea was to set fire to the rope which would then ignite a fire from the fuel tank. This idea was of course unsuccessful.

"These were hair-brained schemes from the start," Russo said, "particularly the fuel tank episode. What is interesting is that these are passive attacks. There is no face to face encounter with the mother, they just really want her gone. But it does show how these were test-runs of sorts. Sullivan was working up his nerve to do something violent. Nicole was building up her psyche. With each unsuccessful dry run, their determination and focus to do the job became greater until finally they realized that physical violence would be the only alternative."

THE ATTACK

The couple decided that Sullivan would do the killing. Nicole waited in the car at a local 7-Eleven where he mother worked part time to make ends meet. She wanted to wait there because she hated her home so much. Her boyfriend obliged, and entered the home of Jeanne Domenico between the hours of six and seven in the evening, waiting for her to come home from work.

The plan was for Billy to kill Jeanne by hitting her on the back of her head with a baseball bat.

Nicole waited anxiously in the car for an extended period of time then began to get worried as to why Sullivan was taking so long.

"Nicole called him and asked him what was taking so long," Wilson said. "Jeanne began getting upset that Nicole wasn't home and kept saying 'where is she? Tell her to come home.'"

Nicole heard her mother's voice on the other end of her cell phone telling her to "come home."

As became her habit, she did not listen to her mother.

"Sullivan did not attack Jeanne immediately," Russo said. "Again, he needed that fuel to add to his fire. So he confronted Jeanne, asking her why they kept refusing them to be together. Jeanne would speak logically like any adult would. She's underage. She's still in school. Of course, none of this would get into the head of Sullivan."

Jeanne made the mistake of turning her back on the young man. He then hit her across the back with the baseball bat.

"It looks as if Jeanne tried to get out of the kitchen door," Wilson said. "Billy started grabbing kitchen knives and attacking Jeanne with the steak knives from the state clock in the kitchen."

The attack was, in a word, brutal.

Sullivan stabbed Jeanne numerous times near her heart and stomach. He stabbed with such ferocity that the blade broke off the knife and he had to retrieve another. Then he stabbed her eight times in the throat.

"A number of the steak knives snapped off during the course of the attack," Wilson said.

According to later testimony by Sullivan, Jeanne managed to get a hold of one of the knives and tried to fight back. At this point, however, she is stunned and bleeding. Sullivan realizes that he is in trouble and goes in to finish the job.

Sullivan stabs her repeatedly as Jeanne tries to get away. A blade enters her lung.

"I'm done," were Jeanne's final words.

He then changed his clothes and cleaned the blood off. He then went back to Nicole, telling her to go inside the house to check for any weapons that he may have left behind. He also told her to get a towel.

The murder complete, Sullivan returned to the vehicle and announced that he had done the deal.

The couple, however, had a deal. It was now time for Nicole to do her part. She would help clean up the evidence left behind.

"The fact that she could go and clean up after Billy had killed her mother," Wilson said. "She had to have hit her mother with the door. And then she had to have stepped over her body to clean up for her boyfriend. That she was able to do that was chilling to do me."

Nicole took a cloth and began clean up her mother's blood from the kitchen floor.

"The fact that a psychopath like Sullivan was able to stab Jeanne to death isn't the most blood curdling aspect of this case," Russo said. "The really scary part is how Nicole was able to go back into that house, see her mother laying in a pool of blood on the kitchen floor, then begin to do her end of the bargain, which was to clean up after her boyfriend. The amount of psychological and emotional disconnect here is chilling."

The two then hid the evidence in the outskirts around town before going to a shopping mall in order for Sullivan to purchase new clothes.

Hours after the killing, Nicole finally began to realize the gravity of what has taken place. She realizes that she and Billy were not going off to "see the world." Her best friend, her mother was gone forever.

Jeanne's body would be discovered by her boyfriend later that evening and he quickly called the police. At around 10:15 p.m., Sergeant William Moore and Detective Shawn Hill saw Sullivan and Nicole approach the crime scene.

"They were cocky enough to think they could outwit the cops," Russo said. "By approaching the crime scene and acting all innocent, not knowing what happened, they thought they would deflect attention away from themselves. It really shows you how dumb these two kids were."

The police then stated the teens would have to be separated for an interview. Nicole protested, stating that Sullivan would not know how to get to the police station. The police informed her that they would take him there themselves.

"This is when things start to go haywire in their heads," Russo said. "Nicole is getting nervous, knowing that they will be questioned separately and face the prospect of not having their stories straight. These two were not exactly forward thinking individuals."

The two waited for the police cruisers to arrive and made conversation with Detective Moore. The detective noted that Sullivan did most all of the talking and admitted that he did not like police officers, stating that he had been charged before with crimes he did not commit.

Moore informed Sullivan that he would be given a "fair shake" in the questioning.

Sullivan, however, kept talking. He informed the detective that he had been shopping for souvenirs with Nicole that day and talked about Jeanne's relationship with Nicole. The detective said that Sullivan paced back and forth and then sat down on the trunk of his car.

Twelve minutes later, Detective Linehan arrived on the scene, making contact with both Nicole and Sullivan. Linehan noticed how nervous and "jumpy" Sullivan was. Linehan told Sullivan to "relax" and then the teen explained that he suffered from anxiety but did not need medication. He told the police that he had "no problem" to come to the station for questioning.

Linehan sat with Sullivan in the back seat of the squad car as they headed back to the station. Both of the teens were having casual conversations with the officers but after being questioned separately, they both admitted their involvement, leading police to the locations where they had disposed of the evidence.

"Both of the teenage lovers wilted under the police interrogations," Russo said. "She immediately ratted out Sullivan as the killer while he did the same to her. There was no loyalty for one another while under the police questioning."

Sullivan would be convicted of first degree murder, sentenced to life without parole.

Sullivan, however, did not let his Lothario ways go to rust in jail. He wrote love letters to a girl named Monique Teal who was then sixteen. This occurred while Sullivan was awaiting trial and later Teal's testimony was used in court.

Teal, using a pen name of Monique Sullivan in her love letters to Sullivan, had agreed to a date to marry the now twenty-year old murderer. Teal's mother, however, found out about the letters and forbade him to call or write.

"He just laughed about it," she said. "He said that no matter what my mom would say or do that nothing could keep us away from each other."

"You see him trying the same techniques on Teal," Russo said. "The immediate declarations of love. The flowery language. The idea of them against the world. In Teal's case, however, her mother put a stop to it."

Sullivan admitted to the Jeanne Domenico killing in one of his letters to her, Teal would reveal, although she didn't read from the letter in court. She said she obeyed Sullivan's demands and threw that letter away.

JAIL LIFE

Nicole Kasinskas would plead guilty to second-degree murder.

"My original sentence was forty years to life," Nicole said. "It is now thirty-seven years and a half to life based on a plea that if I acquired my GED I would get two and a half years off. I don't mark days off on my calendar. I don't do those types of things. This is my life now and I want to live it. I don't want to just look at it as one day down closer to my real life. Like this is my real life. I smile a lot and I live a lot and I'm happy a lot and I just prefer it that way rather than get lost in the sadness of it because you can. And I have. But if I...if I can choose not to...if I can be stronger than than then I want to. And it makes me feel freer. It makes me feel that I have more control of my life."

"Her life as a promising honor roll student at fifteen years old with her mother who loved her very much," Wilson said. "She lost her entire life. And for what?"

"I had no goals. I had no hopes and dreams, you know? You need to have your own hobbies and friends and stuff. Outside the relationship, there needs to be that balance. I just never had that, I never figured that out."

"Maybe if someone had said something like, 'I see you, I see that there's more to you than this and I want to see more of you. I'm here for you. I care about you.' I mean everyone needs help, everyone needs support."

A MOTHER'S KILLER : THE TRUE STORY OF JENNIFER BAILEY

AMBER ULLMER

Imagine coming home after a hard day of work through the door to your quarter of a million dollar home. Then, hearing an eerie silence and nothing but darkness surrounding every inch of your four bedroom, two bathroom, roomy home. With a passing glance to the dining room and living room of your 3400-square-foot house, you head up the stairs with the goal of taking a warm bath and getting a fresh set of clothes for the night.

This is what Susan Bailey[1] did just before it happened. Two dozen stab wounds and two slashes to her throat cut that goal short with a spattering of blood on the wall and a coagulating pool of blood beneath her. She didn't expect to be killed that night. Neither did she expect it to be her own children who would do it to her.

Susan Marie Bailey grew up as a bubbly, funny, outgoing, and smart kid, according to her mother, Kate Morten. She had curly dark hair, was the second of four kids, and was extremely musically talented with the violin and clarinet. Susan was always a people-person. She wanted to do something at the intersection of business, fashion, and people. So, she went to college and earned a business and accounting degree at her local Minnesota college.

---

1. http://www.apple.com/

To get her fashion experience, Susan worked at Levi Strauss & Co. while in college. She still wanted to get out there more. Her life was a struggle in Minnesota with the snow stomping on her every attempt to be successful. She couldn't make it to work during the winter and work didn't stop just for the weather.

Susan had a difficult time commuting to work. She had to struggle through twenty miles of snow and ice every day. Months and months of brutal winter weather created snow drifts and blinding blizzards that became a routine. She requested to be moved to a closer store which they allowed her to do. Even though it became easier because she didn't have to drive that far in that bad of weather through the winter, it wasn't any easier in the Spring. An extra 28 inches of snow replaced pleasant Spring weather.

Then, one time when she had to close up shop after the other customers left and the cleaning had been done, she locked the front door and discovered an empty parking lot. Well, almost empty. Snow took over everything in sight, including her car.

Snow chilled her to the bone, darkness swallowed the town, and she was all alone. The snow was so high that she couldn't even open the doors to her car to get inside. So, she called her parents from a pay phone in a state of panic. She cried and in a fit of shivering from the cold she told her mother, "I'm never going to spend another winter in Minnesota." She did just that.

With that, Susan moved to California and built a successful clothing store. Then, she met her husband, Richard Bailey. Not so long after, she called up her mom with a startling message. "Mom, I'm married," Susan told her mother over a phone call in 1988, "Richard and I eloped."

Richard worked in the military and Susan was forced to follow him around while he was in the military. After he finished with the military, he took over caring for his kids and Susan worked. She worked extremely hard and took good care of her kids: Jennifer and David.

She worked two jobs to make sure that her kids could have anything and everything they ever wanted. Problems started when Jennifer was 18 and she wanted a 16-year-old guy named Paul Henson Jr. He was into Satanism, songs about death, and role-playing games. Of course, Jennifer's mother wasn't so thrilled about this and forbid her daughter to see the boy.

Similarly, 14-year-old Merrilee White wanted to be with Jennifer's boyfriend and she was willing to go to great lengths to do so. Her mother, Amy White, also didn't like Paul and told her not to see him. Meanwhile, little David Bailey just wanted to make his sister happy who oftentimes had to take care of him because the mom worked so much.

According to Donna Fielder, author of "Ladykiller," Paul Henson convinced the two that he had two personalities. Apparently, each girl was dating one of them.

Jennifer was scheduled to begin at an art college in a few days and the other three were supposed to start at Northwest Independent School District. Under the veil of appearing to be innocent teenagers, the four of them plotted for days. They planned on killing their parents so they could all be together, drive to Canada, and live happily ever after.

Paul, a 16-year-old with a double personality in which one was an executioner from the 18th century, had been dying to kill someone anyway. He wanted to know what it was like. So, Merrilee attempted to stab her sleeping mother who luckily talked her out of trying to stab her, Paul waited at home with a gun for his parents, and Jennifer Bailey waited at home for her hard-working mom to get home so she could kill her.

Jennifer Bailey was the only successful one out of the three. Susan Bailey was just coming home after leaving her second job in Fort Worth, Texas for the day. She returned home just in time. Jen, Paul, and David took turns stabbing Susan 26 times[2] in the throat after Paul's attempt to kill his parents didn't work.

On September 29, 2008, 11:31 AM, it was reported that 43-year-old Susan Bailey was found dead in her Roanoke home. The Tarrant County Medical Examiner's office claimed that she had multiple stab wounds to her neck. According to star-telegram.com[3], "Sgt. Chris Almonrode said officers had visited her home in the 200 block of Oxford Drive on Friday at the request of the woman's mother, who had grown concerned after not hearing from her daughter. He said officers could not get an answer at the door and found no evidence indicating that anything was wrong."

Kate Morten, Susan's mother, tried calling her daughter from her home in Minnesota. When no one answered, she called the Roanoke, Texas police. No one came to the door of their upscale home, so the Roanoke police burst into the door and found a murder scene.

They found the mother's body upstairs in the hallway sitting in a pool of her own blood. Foul play was immediately suspected as the cause of death. The Texas officers also found a bowl of poisoned pudding, a chunk of hair, and an electrical cord dangling right into a bathtub. Inside the bathtub sat three phones and a knife under a foot of water. Jennifer and David were going to kill their mother one way or another.

Meanwhile, a curious South Dakota cop [4]stopped Susan's car for violating town curfew and couldn't believe what he found. He pulled over Jennifer Bailey, 14-year-old David, and 16-year-old Paul in Susan's 2002 Saturn. He pulled them over at a closed gas station where they were trying to steal gas. They didn't have any money and their stories didn't make much sense. They had no real plan either.

---

2.   http://donnakayefielder.blogspot.com/

3.   http://star-telegram.com/

4.   http://www.apple.com/

He took them to the station and called the police in Roanoke, Texas. They knew about the kids and the woman that the car was registered to. The Tuesday before that week, Paul's father reported him a runaway and thought he was at Jennifer's house. The officers did not find him there. They did find his packed bags and a driver's license. Later on that day, they came back when Susan found a loaded magazine for a pistol, but the police couldn't find the gun.

Roanoke officers quickly put the pieces together after hearing that the three were together in Susan's car. At first, they didn't go straight in when the mother called worried about Susan because no one came to the door and the car was gone. When they found out about the kids, that's when they went in through the house through a window and found the dead mother.

The officer called Roanoke police and upon hearing what was happening, he held the three on suspicion of capital murder. They were all held at a juvenile detention facility in Sioux Falls, S.D.

Paul wasn't able to kill his parents, they decided to stay out late for a dinner and a movie, thankfully. Merrilee White, on the other hand, didn't get to kill her mother Amy White because luckily, she woke up before she could. The 15-year-old Fort Worth girl was detained on the 23rd of September after her mother reported that she woke up and found the girl standing over her with a knife. Merrilee was demanding that Amy give her her car keys. The girl later admitted to the police that she wanted to take her mother's car so that could take her friends to Canada.

When authorities went to investigate[5], they found notebooks, binders, and handwritten papers, computers, and discs that police described as, "pertaining to the preparation of murder." In the boyfriend's home, they found handwritten notes, papers, computers, discs, and "The Demonic Bible." As mentioned earlier, Paul loved to

---

5.   http://www.nbcdfw.com/news/local/

Affidavits_4_Teens_Planned_To_Kill_N_Texas_Mom.html

practice Satanism and was fond of all the things any parents wouldn't want their 17-year-old to be into. He was an avid fan of role-playing and fantasized frequently. Only, this wasn't done as a result of the fantasizing mind of a deranged 17-year-old; it was real.

On September 23rd, police called the Bailey home because they were looking for the boyfriend who was reported as a runaway. Susan and Jennifer fought over Paul. Police later came back later when Susan reported finding ammunition. The police searched the home and found a butcher knife in between the couch cushions and a knife under Jennifer's bed. Jennifer was showing signs of plans to kill early enough that it could have been prevented. However, her sweet mother had no clue that Jen would actually kill her.

Their school district, Northwest Independent School District, commented on this in an article published on September 29th in 2008 at approximately 11:31 AM. They said, "Our thoughts are with the families involved, and our school personnel continue to focus on the education and well being of our students. Should any child or staff member need to talk about the situation, school counselors are available." Too bad their counselors didn't notice earlier how unstable these four children were. Susan Bailey might still be alive.

Donna Fielder, as mentioned later, spoke to Kate, Susan's mom, who said that she still couldn't believe that her grandchildren would do such a terrible thing. Kate lived through the moment with baited breath from the phone call that drew silence from her deceased daughter to the announcement that her grandchildren killed their mother, her daughter.

What happened to the other three kids? [6]Jen stayed in the Denton County jail without bail and the boys stayed at the Denton Country Juvenile Facility. All three faced capital murder charges. They even tried to try Paul as an adult. In this case, he would serve out his Juvenile

---

6.   http://www.nbcdfw.com/news/local/

Affidavits_4_Teens_Planned_To_Kill_N_Texas_Mom.html

sentence and then finish up his sentence as an adult afterward. Under normal conditions[7], juvenile offenders were released from Texas Youth Commission when they would become adults so they could serve out the rest of their sentence. Davide was tried under state's determinate sentencing statute.

Paul got 60 years in prison[8], Jennifer got 60 years in prison, and David only did his juvenile term then went on to live as normal a life as he could have. When police asked Jennifer about her motive, she simply said, "We did not see eye to eye."

It seems like such a small charge for murderers. Would a life-sentence have been more deserved? Probably. Did they get a light charge because they were only kids? Most likely.

My Life of Crime [9]laid out the details in regards to the three murderers. Jennifer Bailey is a white female born on October 5th, 1990. Her maximum sentence date is September, 26th, 2068 which she has been sentenced to spend at Hilltop Unit. Hilltop Unit[10]. is a correctional institutions division (prison) located at 1500 State School Road, Gatesville, TX 76598-2996. It can be found three miles outside of Gatesville.

On The Texas Tribune[11], Jennifer Bailey is listed as being located at the Mountain View Unit for committing "LESSER INCLU MURDER committed on 9/26/2008 in Denton County" for which she is serving a "60-year term" beginning on "9/26/1008."

---

7.   http://crimeblog.dallasnews.com/2008/12/roanoke-woman-indicted-in-moth.html/

8.   http://www.apple.com/

9.   https://mylifeofcrime.wordpress.com/2012/12/07/kids-that-kill-jennifer-bailey-david-bailey-and-paul-allen-henson-jr/

10.   https://www.tdcj.state.tx.us/unit_directory/ht.html

11.   https://www.texastribune.org/library/data/texas-prisons/inmates/jennifer-bailey/727001/

She is listed as a female, at 25 years of age, found in Mountain View under 01621147, from Denton county, and born 10/5/1990. She is white, 5 ft 5 in, 122 lbs, with blonde hair and hazel eyes.

Her parole eligibility date is 9/26/2038.

On *Denton County, TX Jail Records*, Paul Allen Henson Jr. is listed with the aliases of "Talos, Malaki, and Scai" with an SO# of 164000, and he is described as a white male with brown hair/eyes standing 6'3" at 145 pounds. He was booked at the Denton County Sheriff's Office on 06/09/2009 for capital murder by terror threat/other felony. His offense date is 09/26/2008. Because he has to spend 60 years in jail, he's looking to be released 9/26/2068.

A few years later, Candice Delong sat down in an interview with Jennifer Bailey for the details on Jennifer's perspective that night when they killed Susan Bailey.

During the video,[12] Jennifer says that she went upstairs and started feeling doubtful. She went upstairs to the bathroom and looked at herself good in the face. Jennifer knew she would have to look at that face for the rest of her life and the decision she was about to make.

She questioned if she really wanted to kill her mother. She explained, "That is when I made the decision that I was going to tell my mom what was going to happen and then call the police regardless of the consequences." She then said that she was too late. She heard a scream that broke her thought processes. She went out to the hallway and found her mother pushed up against the wall by Paul who had one hand around her throat and a knife in the other.

Jennifer Bailey then says that her mother told her to "call the police." She adds, "Then I said no."

Explaining why, she said, "Because, at the same time, Paul pointed at me and said, 'Don't!' And to this day, I have no idea why I said, 'no.' After I said, 'no,' Paul just grins and pulls the knife across her throat." From there, Jennifer and David helped finish the mother off. With

---

12.   http://www.investigationdiscovery.com/tv-shows/facing-evil/videos/jennifer-bailey/

that, they took off with the mother's car, no money, and whatever gas was in the tank to get them to Canada.

Donna Fielder, the woman who originally covered this story when working at the local newspaper in the Bailey's hometown, recalls the event in September 2008 that ended with the death of Susan Bailey at the hands of four teenagers. She explains how the four of them: Jennifer Bailey, David Bailey, Paul Henson, and Merrilee White tried to kill their parents and steal whatever money they could from them before taking their cars they planned on driving all the way to Canada from Texas.

She recalls that the four teenagers plotted against Susan Bailey, a hard-working mother, and the long journey they made from her death to that run-down gas station they were pulled over at.

Jennifer Bailey, David Bailey, Merrilee White, and Paul Allen Henson enacted one of the most violent crimes in US history to a woman who did not deserve such an attack. It was such a popular case that filmmakers have taken to the story and made video-enactments of it such as *Deadly Women,* a series that took Jennifer Bailey's story and portrayed her as a young girl who fell in love with a pagan, Paul. Paul convinces Bailey to kill her mother and run off with him. They plan on running off to Canada together, but it doesn't quite go as planned. The mother tells her they cannot speak and havoc wreaks as Paul tells Jennifer that she needs to brutally murder her mother.

Susan Bailey was a hard working mother of Jennifer and David who had anything and everything they ever wanted until Paul came into the picture and what they had was just not enough.

Jennifer and Merrilee were bound so tight under the spell of Paul and David just wanted to make his sister happy. With that, they took a sharp blade and took away Susan's life and breath. They tried to get away and enjoy a happy life in the cold of Canada, but they lacked a plan and cash to make that fantasy a truth.

Perhaps this was all the will of a psychopathic teenager who thought he was two people. Sadly, he ruined the lives of two young girls and a young boy to fulfill his disgusting fantasies.

To this day, David and Merrilee sit alone and forgotten and without the ones they loved. Jennifer and Paul await 52 years more of time to stare at bars and cement walls. David lost a sister, a mother, and two friends. Merrilee lost three friends and the trust of her mother. Paul lost two loving parents and both his girlfriends. Jennifer lost the most: her boyfriend who she cared for dearly, her mother, and her self-worth.

The moral of the story? The all-American family, neighbors, children aren't all that movies and books make them be. Darkness taints the pages of every good storybook.

A MOTHER'S KILLER :

THE TRUE STORY OF NICOLE KASINSKAS

42

CHRISTINE GOODMAN

Nicole Kasinskas was a quiet, unassuming teenage girl. She was born and raised in Nashua, New Hampshire to Anthony Kasinskas and Jeanne Domenico.

"I lived with both of my parents and my younger brother until I was eleven years old," Nicole said. "And my parents divorced and my Dad moved out."

"I think after my parents got divorced and I was dealing with that, I became a little bit angrier. I had a little bit more resentment towards him, and it did change my perspectives about myself and about life in general, I guess even as an eleven year old."

In May of 2002, she found "romance" as a fifteen year old on-line with eighteen-year old Billy Sullivan.

Sullivan lived in a town called Willmantic where he worked as a line cook at McDonald's.

"Nicole hadn't had a lot of boyfriends," prosecuting attorney Kirsten Wilson said . "She was really caught up by the attention by this guy who was saying amazing things to her about how beautiful she was and what she meant to him."

They would communicate daily through e-mail, letters and phone calls. Despite not having met in person, they both declared love for each other within days, speaking of marriage and planning their future together.

"They filled in sort of the gaps of everyday communication and relationships with fantasies and making these assumptions on who the other person was," Wilson said.

"He lived in Connecticut and so our relationship was almost one hundred percent over the phone," Nicole said. "But it became everything to me very quickly because of the amount of attention that he paid me, and I didn't really feel that I was getting that from anywhere else."

Nicole had been vulnerable to Sullivan's Internet advances as she was a loner with very few friends in high school. She was routinely bullied at school by other girls. On one occasion, she was walking down the hall and one of her bullies had pulled her sweatpants down to her ankles. Nicole was not wearing any underwear, furthering the humiliation. Nicole refused to go back to school the next day after that incident.

"The bullying at school certainly made Nicole vulnerable to someone like Sullivan," forensic psychologist Fiona Russo said. "She's lonely, she's being picked on at school and completely humiliated. She stuck to herself and so when some guy pays attention to her, even when it is only online, her fantasy life goes into overdrive. She's able to project things on him that he doesn't deserve or merit."

The more severe the bullying became, the more Nicole began to withdraw and cling to Sullivan.

"As I got older, it was easier for me to isolate from people," Nicole said. "I think at that point I had just gotten used to being more alone as opposed to being around people. And it just became a part of who I was. Maybe if I was more open or maybe if someone had tried harder to reach out, that it could've been different."

Nicole's mom, Jeanne, was her best friend. Jeanne worked at an elementary school for a period of time, holding down such jobs as a crossing guard, a lunchroom monitor, and a paraprofessional for about three years before taking a job where she worked on group contracts for the Benefits, Brokers and Administration department.

"Jeanne Domenico was well loved in the community," Wilson said. "Hard worker. Really sort of a bright, energetic, sweet woman. She was trying to make her daughter happy."

Despite the bullying at school, Nicole got straight A's at school and made her mother happy whenever she made the honor roll.

"School really became my self-worth and I really identified with, like whatever my grades were," Nicole said. "However I was doing in school I felt it reflected on me personally, because I felt that it was so much a part of who I was. I never got in trouble in middle school. I never got spoken to. I never had a detention. It never really crossed my mind to do anything that would be against the rules."

"It would have been helpful if there was more of an acknowledgment that I was doing so well. I think it also would've been helpful if there was more involvement with guidance or something. Just more of a like a check-in...see how things are going."

"Somehow, someway, Nicole got lost in the cracks," Russo said. "That in no way justifies what she did. It may be how she justified it during this time. Her parents are divorced. She doesn't see her Dad. Her mom is working all the time. There had to have been days where she felt intense loneliness Going to school just to be ignored or bullied. To a fourteen year old girl you really may not see the light at the end of the tunnel. So you seek an outlet. Some turn to drugs. Nicole found her own drug in the form of the words that came out of Sullivan's keyboard."

MOTHER AND DAUGHTER TROUBLES

At least on the surface, there were no problems between mother and daughter.

Until Nicole ventured on-line and met Billy Sullivan.

Her mother found out about the relationship and wanting to make her daughter happy, drove the young teenager out to Connecticut so she could meet Sullivan for the first time.

"This was a two hour drive from Nashua to the place in Connecticut where Sullivan lived," Russo said. "It is easy to say here is where Jeanne made a fatal mistake. But in her mind, it is all innocent. Her daughter is fourteen and begging her to drive out to meet this guy. Begging and begging. Until she finally she relents."

More visits followed but friends and classmates knew little of the teen's relationship. Sullivan had informed some of his friends that he had a girlfriend that was "out of state." Other than that, he revealed very little about his personal life.

"He's quiet, he didn't really like to talk," recalled Danny Goss who was a classmate of Sullivan. "But he was good in school and didn't get in any trouble."

"I think the relationship intensified to a degree that Jeanne herself didn't anticipate," Russo said. "And it is easy to play Monday morning quarterback here but there had to have been some kind of father figure present to say 'hey, this is an eighteen-year old working at McDonald's. You are a fourteen year old honor student. You have a future. Don't blow it on this guy. But it isn't like teens listen to you anyway."

The two teenagers soon discussed the prospect of moving in together. Her mother quickly objected to this idea as well as nixing the idea of Nicole sharing a joint bank account with Sullivan.

But the young man later stayed overnight one weekend with Nicole's mother's full consent.

The relationship is the first for Nicole. She pedestalizes Sullivan as everything she has fantasized about is coming true.

"Nicole had a void in her life," Russo said. "When her parents divorced it certainly affected her psychologically in the way she viewed men. Then along comes Sullivan whose older and more experienced. She gets the love from him that perhaps she sought from her father. The older man, wiser than his years, showering her with attention. She was vulnerable to that."

"Her father didn't have too much to do with her after the divorce. She had that longing in her heart for that male figure. And along came Sullivan."

PERSONAL DEMONS OF HIS OWN

Sullivan, however, had his own personal demons he was fighting.

"He did have mental health issues," Wilson said. "He had been hospitalized a number of times. During high school he had some behavioral issues. Some anxiety, that kind of thing."

It was later revealed that Sullivan had been on numerous psychiatric medications to curb his depression, anger and schizophrenia. He had been weaning himself off the meds, however, and on one occasion he engaged in an argument with Nicole's mother over dinner.

Jeanne had asked Billy if she liked the dinner she had prepared. He said yes and then Jean made the comment that "I bet you don't get that too much at home."

Sullivan was highly defensive over anything that involved his home life. When Jeanne made that comment, he turned hostile.

"Sullivan was protective of his home life," Russo said. "If anyone insulted his mother or if he even perceives that someone is insulting his mother then he gets abusive. He did this to Jeanne, who had obviously made nothing more than an idle comment. That was the first warning sign and the relationship should have ended then and there."

Nicole, however, defended her young beau and from that moment the tug of war for her heart began.

"Nicole's own naivete comes to bore at this point," Russo said. "She has no experience with boys and here is this older guy that she looks up to, almost as a father figure of sorts, who turns her against her own family. Against the one person who loved her the most. Her mother. It is a tug of war that the mother loses simply because her daughter's hormones are raging and she doesn't yet have the emotional capacity to know any better."

After a year of dating, in August of 2003, Sullivan drove out to Nashua to spend a week with Nicole. By this time, they are both fed up with Nicole's mother's objections to their ideas of cohabitation.

"Our relationship was definitely emotionally abusive," Nicole said. "And I think now over time, from looking at it, my perspectives on that have changed so much. I feel like he is responsible for his actions and I am responsible for mine. I didn't really get that and I feel like in order to be emotionally abused, in order to stand for it and stay in it, there's gotta be something missing in you. There's gotta be something hurting already, something is not there, something's not right. And that needs to be figured out, found and fixed. Regardless of how a child is acting or what's coming off, there's more inside that kids need help with or guidance or just to have some type of connection with someone. You need to have relationships with people ahead of time, so that when the bad stuff does happen does happen you don't just come in to it expecting to work it out. Like, you need to have firm foundation with that person in order to work it out."

Nicole continued to side with Sullivan against her mother. The two argued constantly, Sullivan's influence quickly become apparent in Nicole's attitude toward her mother as she found fault with everything she did.

The two teens began discussing an unheard of option.

They began discussing the prospect of killing her mother.

"Well, this is where it starts getting…it's a scary business for me," Nicole said in a jailhouse interview. "I'll tell you that. I feel like I"m gonna cry. I don't talk about this stuff so this is really the first time. I think that my relationship with my mom was good. It was fine. I loved my mom. And…that changed. When…I'm not saying I stopped loving my mom, but…our relationship changed. I'm not gonna say that we were the most open because we weren't. We didn't talk about every little thing. I don't remember ever once talking about my parents' divorce with either of them. But the thing is, we didn't really talk about much of anything. When I was fourteen, I became involved with seventeen year old boy. This is really stemming into why I'm here (in jail) now."

OUT OF CONTROL

"Emotions begin to run high as Sullivan ups the ante in his hatred for Nicole's mother," Russo said. "Nicole is emotionally underdeveloped and has to choose between her mother and her 'man.' It is easy to look at it hindsight but with the teenaged girl's warp logic, she sees Sullivan as her entire world now. So she will do anything for him. Even murder."

Nicole's mom really didn't realize the danger that Sullivan was. She began doing what every mom does, demanding that her daughter stop seeing him, stop chatting with him and concentrate on her schoolwork. Nicole, on the other hand, remained fervent in her desire to move to Connecticut to move in with Sullivan.

"Jeanie, rightfully so, said 'you're fifteen you're finishing school,'" Wilson said. "'You're not moving to Connecticut' and that really upset both Nicole and Billy."

The prospect of not seeing Nicole had an adverse emotional effect on Billy.

"He started talking about killing himself...on the road...driving into a big truck because of leaving me..because of his sadness over it," Nicole recalled. "And I think now it just sounds silly, you know? But it wasn't then, and it was terrifying to me because I didn't...I didn't know how to...because of the way that our relationship was. Because he had become so much a part of my life. I mean, I really didn't feel like I was anything without him. I had nothing in my life at that time...I felt...at that time. So the thought of losing him in that way just wasn't okay with me. And that is unfortunately when conversations started about ultimately what happened. I guess I really I don't really go into too many details but I was sixteen and he was eighteen at that time. And I guess I should give you some background. He killed my mom and I was a part of it. I was not physically there but I knew and I helped him. I was, you know, going through the motions of what was being done. But mentally and emotionally, I don't think I was fully there. I don't think I was fully getting it."

"It was emotional manipulation," Russo said. "It is all so scary romantic for a fifteen year old girl to have some guy who is so in love with her that he is going to kill himself because he can't be with her. She has no one in her life to say 'this guy is a loser nutcase.' There isn't anyone that can talk sense to her. So she falls for the emotional manipulation of a highly disturbed but cunning con man."

Billy had convinced the depressed Nicole that her mother was an obstacle to both hers and his happiness.

"I really just did whatever I could to maintain that relationship because I didn't want to lose that," Nicole said. "I didn't want to lose him. And I quickly learned how it would go if I didn't always do everything that he wanted me to do. At that point...you know, getting to be fifteen...sixteen years old...I would fight more with my mom and there was a lot more to fight about, especially with, you know, this relationship that I was having with this kid."

THE FINAL PLAN

The couple tried different methods to murder Jeanne Domenico.

First they tried to poison Jeanne's coffee. The teens had placed Dimetapp, Benadryl and other drugs into Jeanne's coffee creamer in the refrigerator.

Jeanne used the creamer but didn't die and evidently remained ignorant of the plot on her life. The teens then added bleach to the creamer, wanting to strengthen the amount of poison. It was unclear in a court affidavit if Jeanne ever drank from the spiked creamer again.

The next idea was to set Nicole's mattress on fire with a candle. That idea didn't work because the bedding was made of fire retardant material.

It is unclear how the teens planned to fire up the mattress, whether they sneaked into her Nicole's bedroom and tried to fire up the mattress while she slept.

The third idea was to blow up the fuel oil tank in Jeanne's house. The teens had tied two ropes together which would serve as a wick. Their idea was to set fire to the rope which would then ignite a fire from the fuel tank. This idea was of course unsuccessful.

"These were hair-brained schemes from the start," Russo said, "particularly the fuel tank episode. What is interesting is that these are passive attacks. There is no face to face encounter with the mother, they just really want her gone. But it does show how these were test-runs of sorts. Sullivan was working up his nerve to do something violent. Nicole was building up her psyche. With each unsuccessful dry run, their determination and focus to do the job became greater until finally they realized that physical violence would be the only alternative."

THE ATTACK

The couple decided that Sullivan would do the killing. Nicole waited in the car at a local 7-Eleven where he mother worked part time to make ends meet. She wanted to wait there because she hated her home so much. Her boyfriend obliged, and entered the home of Jeanne Domenico between the hours of six and seven in the evening, waiting for her to come home from work.

The plan was for Billy to kill Jeanne by hitting her on the back of her head with a baseball bat.

Nicole waited anxiously in the car for an extended period of time then began to get worried as to why Sullivan was taking so long.

"Nicole called him and asked him what was taking so long," Wilson said. "Jeanne began getting upset that Nicole wasn't home and kept saying 'where is she? Tell her to come home.'"

Nicole heard her mother's voice on the other end of her cell phone telling her to "come home."

As became her habit, she did not listen to her mother.

"Sullivan did not attack Jeanne immediately," Russo said. "Again, he needed that fuel to add to his fire. So he confronted Jeanne, asking her why they kept refusing them to be together. Jeanne would speak logically like any adult would. She's underage. She's still in school. Of course, none of this would get into the head of Sullivan."

Jeanne made the mistake of turning her back on the young man. He then hit her across the back with the baseball bat.

"It looks as if Jeanne tried to get out of the kitchen door," Wilson said. "Billy started grabbing kitchen knives and attacking Jeanne with the steak knives from the state clock in the kitchen."

The attack was, in a word, brutal.

Sullivan stabbed Jeanne numerous times near her heart and stomach. He stabbed with such ferocity that the blade broke off the knife and he had to retrieve another. Then he stabbed her eight times in the throat.

"A number of the steak knives snapped off during the course of the attack," Wilson said.

According to later testimony by Sullivan, Jeanne managed to get a hold of one of the knives and tried to fight back. At this point, however, she is stunned and bleeding. Sullivan realizes that he is in trouble and goes in to finish the job.

Sullivan stabs her repeatedly as Jeanne tries to get away. A blade enters her lung.

"I'm done," were Jeanne's final words.

He then changed his clothes and cleaned the blood off. He then went back to Nicole, telling her to go inside the house to check for any weapons that he may have left behind. He also told her to get a towel.

The murder complete, Sullivan returned to the vehicle and announced that he had done the deal.

The couple, however, had a deal. It was now time for Nicole to do her part. She would help clean up the evidence left behind.

"The fact that she could go and clean up after Billy had killed her mother," Wilson said. "She had to have hit her mother with the door. And then she had to have stepped over her body to clean up for her boyfriend. That she was able to do that was chilling to do me."

Nicole took a cloth and began clean up her mother's blood from the kitchen floor.

"The fact that a psychopath like Sullivan was able to stab Jeanne to death isn't the most blood curdling aspect of this case," Russo said. "The really scary part is how Nicole was able to go back into that house, see her mother laying in a pool of blood on the kitchen floor, then begin to do her end of the bargain, which was to clean up after her boyfriend. The amount of psychological and emotional disconnect here is chilling."

The two then hid the evidence in the outskirts around town before going to a shopping mall in order for Sullivan to purchase new clothes.

Hours after the killing, Nicole finally began to realize the gravity of what has taken place. She realizes that she and Billy were not going off to "see the world." Her best friend, her mother was gone forever.

Jeanne's body would be discovered by her boyfriend later that evening and he quickly called the police. At around 10:15 p.m., Sergeant William Moore and Detective Shawn Hill saw Sullivan and Nicole approach the crime scene.

"They were cocky enough to think they could outwit the cops," Russo said. "By approaching the crime scene and acting all innocent, not knowing what happened, they thought they would deflect attention away from themselves. It really shows you how dumb these two kids were."

The police then stated the teens would have to be separated for an interview. Nicole protested, stating that Sullivan would not know how to get to the police station. The police informed her that they would take him there themselves.

"This is when things start to go haywire in their heads," Russo said. "Nicole is getting nervous, knowing that they will be questioned separately and face the prospect of not having their stories straight. These two were not exactly forward thinking individuals."

The two waited for the police cruisers to arrive and made conversation with Detective Moore. The detective noted that Sullivan did most all of the talking and admitted that he did not like police officers, stating that he had been charged before with crimes he did not commit.

Moore informed Sullivan that he would be given a "fair shake" in the questioning.

Sullivan, however, kept talking. He informed the detective that he had been shopping for souvenirs with Nicole that day and talked about Jeanne's relationship with Nicole. The detective said that Sullivan paced back and forth and then sat down on the trunk of his car.

Twelve minutes later, Detective Linehan arrived on the scene, making contact with both Nicole and Sullivan. Linehan noticed how nervous and "jumpy" Sullivan was. Linehan told Sullivan to "relax" and then the teen explained that he suffered from anxiety but did not need medication. He told the police that he had "no problem" to come to the station for questioning.

Linehan sat with Sullivan in the back seat of the squad car as they headed back to the station. Both of the teens were having casual conversations with the officers but after being questioned separately, they both admitted their involvement, leading police to the locations where they had disposed of the evidence.

"Both of the teenage lovers wilted under the police interrogations," Russo said. "She immediately ratted out Sullivan as the killer while he did the same to her. There was no loyalty for one another while under the police questioning."

Sullivan would be convicted of first degree murder, sentenced to life without parole.

Sullivan, however, did not let his Lothario ways go to rust in jail. He wrote love letters to a girl named Monique Teal who was then sixteen. This occurred while Sullivan was awaiting trial and later Teal's testimony was used in court.

Teal, using a pen name of Monique Sullivan in her love letters to Sullivan, had agreed to a date to marry the now twenty-year old murderer. Teal's mother, however, found out about the letters and forbade him to call or write.

"He just laughed about it," she said. "He said that no matter what my mom would say or do that nothing could keep us away from each other."

"You see him trying the same techniques on Teal," Russo said. "The immediate declarations of love. The flowery language. The idea of them against the world. In Teal's case, however, her mother put a stop to it."

Sullivan admitted to the Jeanne Domenico killing in one of his letters to her, Teal would reveal, although she didn't read from the letter in court. She said she obeyed Sullivan's demands and threw that letter away.

JAIL LIFE

Nicole Kasinskas would plead guilty to second-degree murder.

"My original sentence was forty years to life," Nicole said. "It is now thirty-seven years and a half to life based on a plea that if I acquired my GED I would get two and a half years off. I don't mark days off on my calendar. I don't do those types of things. This is my life now and I want to live it. I don't want to just look at it as one day down closer to my real life. Like this is my real life. I smile a lot and I live a lot and I'm happy a lot and I just prefer it that way rather than get lost in the sadness of it because you can. And I have. But if I...if I can choose not to...if I can be stronger than than then I want to. And it makes me feel freer. It makes me feel that I have more control of my life."

"Her life as a promising honor roll student at fifteen years old with her mother who loved her very much," Wilson said. "She lost her entire life. And for what?"

"I had no goals. I had no hopes and dreams, you know? You need to have your own hobbies and friends and stuff. Outside the relationship, there needs to be that balance. I just never had that, I never figured that out."

"Maybe if someone had said something like, 'I see you, I see that there's more to you than this and I want to see more of you. I'm here for you. I care about you.' I mean everyone needs help, everyone needs support."

THE SUNSET STRIP KILLER: The True Story of Carol Bundy

57

Jessi Gaines

Born Carol Mary Peters on August, 26, 1942, Carol Bundy's childhood, much like her adulthood, was spent pursuing a desperate need for attention and validation. Bundy's ability to idealize or overlook any unpleasantness made her a perfect victim for manipulators and abusers looking for a potential victim – a talent she picked up early on to deal with the abuses of her parents, Charles and Gladys Peters.

Bundy's memories of her childhood are happy ones – Christmases where her parents refused to let their three children miss out on the special holiday because of a lack of money, or her father's attempt to convince her that the tooth fairy had visited overnight, using a doll's feet to leave footprints through Bundy's bedroom. Bundy's mother worked as a hairdresser, but had previously been a stand-in for tap-dancer Ruby Keeler – and Bundy remembered her as a woman who exuded beauty and glamour.

Bundy, on the other hand, was awkward and unattractive, leading her mother to begin treating her as though she didn't even exist. When she was eight, Bundy came home to a locked door, and no matter how much she cried or begged her mother to let her in, Gladys refused – stating that Bundy was not her daughter. Eventually, Charles persuaded Gladys to let the girl in, but even though Bundy was allowed back into the home, her mother ignored her completely.

However, Charles was not without reproach. Gladys, who had a tendency to beat the children relentlessly with a belt, wasn't permitted to hit Bundy or her siblings – but Charles was fond of using physical abuse to assert his dominance. While Bundy remembers her father's beatings as fitting to the severity of the offense, Charles was an alcoholic who used Gladys' death as an excuse to move his assaults on his daughters from physical to sexual.

For eight months, Charles molested both Bundy and her sister Vicky, telling the girls it was their responsibility to "take their mother's place in his bed." Although Vicky maintains that the sexual abuse continued until Charles remarried, Bundy can only recall one instance where her father molested her – and described him as a good man, who loved her.

When Charles remarried, though, he began abusing Bundy more often – beating her, degrading her, humiliating her. He told her she was stupid and fat, and even that he wanted to kill her and the rest of the family – but he'd only gotten as far as the cat before his new wife had taken away his gun. After staying in foster homes, with their grandmother, and with an uncle, the girls were brought back to live with their father in California.

Desperate measures

At this point, Bundy was willing to do anything to get away from her father – and at the age of 17, she married a 56-year-old alcoholic to try and escape the abuse. Bundy had discovered how to use her sexuality and large breasts to seduce men and receive the attention she so desperately needed – but she was unwilling to prostitute herself for her new husband. When she left him, Bundy took up with another older man, a 32-year-old writer named Richard Geis.

With encouragement from Geis, who appreciated her wit and intelligence, Bundy embarked on a brief but somewhat successful writing career. However, after her father hung himself in 1962, Bundy sought comfort through sexual encounters with women. Bouncing frequently between male lovers and female lovers, Bundy was unable to find a reliable source of the attention she needed, so she eventually returned to Geis and the couple moved to Oregon.

Still, Bundy would occasionally let other men pay her for sex. Instead of urging her to seek counseling, Geis agreed to support Bundy while she attended nursing school in Santa Monica – he would pay for her education as long as she kept her grades up. In fact, Bundy was named class valedictorian when she completed the program in 1968.

It was in nursing school that Bundy met her next husband, Grant. Their relationship started off well, and continued to be relatively stable until the birth of their first son – but then, Bundy claimed, he started beating and belittling her. By the time Bundy had given birth to their second son, her eyesight had deteriorated to the point where it looked like she may have to give up nursing. Grant was faced with the prospect of being saddled with the responsibility of caring for a blind wife, as well as their two children, and grew increasingly more violent.

Bundy escaped the abusive marriage and took her two boys to a womens' shelter in 1979, where she stayed for two weeks before finding a small apartment in Van Nuys. The managers of the Valerio Gardens apartment building, Jeanette and John "Jack" Murray, took pity on the poor single mother, and Jack was frequently called on to help Bundy with issues at the apartment. Despite her husband's established pattern of cheating, Jeanette wasn't concerned about the 36-year-old month – Bundy was overweight with short brown hair, a stark contrast to Murray's typical blonde, long-legged mistresses.

The object of her affection

The kindness she saw from Murray led Bundy to develop a crush on her landlord, who took her to the Social Security office so she could receive disability payments and even to the optometrist, to get her fitted for a pair of glasses to help the single mother return to work. Murray, for his part, enjoyed having a captive audience. Good looking, with a fantastic voice, Murray had come to America from Australia to pursue a career in music – but had been unable to make it as a performer thanks to his arrogant attitude.

The two found exactly what they needed in each other, and soon began a sexual relationship. Bundy's crush rapidly became an obsession, and she started coming up with more frequent excuses to have her landlord visit her property. Her infatuation for Murray convinced Bundy that he was in love with her, too – even though he told her it would be years before he would be able to leave his wife. Bundy was well-versed in the art of overlooking negative or painful thoughts and feelings, and continued to look for ways to strengthen the connection she saw with Murray.

Regularly, Bundy loaned her landlord money and bought him expensive gifts after she received the settlement from the sale of the house she'd owned with Grant. She also opened a joint safety deposit box with Murray, and made deposits to help him cover the expenses he said he was incurring as a result of his wife's alleged cancer treatments. Still, Murray wasn't giving Bundy the attention she craved, and she started up a brief affair with Jeanette's younger brother.

In an attempt to spend some time alone with her lover, Bundy arranged a weekend for her and Murray in Las Vegas – as a "reward" for all of his help, she said. However, after the couple checked in at the hotel and took in a show, Murray left Bundy alone for the remainder of the weekend while he gambled. He returned in time to fly back with Bundy, and, hurt and upset, Bundy forgot her suitcase in Murray's van.

When Jeanette showed up at Bundy's door with the forgotten suitcase, Bundy used the opportunity to try and bring her affair with Murray to his wife's attention – thinking Murray would then be forced to leave his wife and finally be with Bundy. During their discussion, Bundy learned that Jeanette never had cancer, and she immediately confronted Murray. While Bundy was initially angry to learn that the money she'd given him to pay for the treatments had actually been used to pay off Murray's van, he calmed her down by reassuring her that his intention was still to leave his wife and eventually be with Bundy. Eventually.

However, Bundy was losing her patience. On Christmas Day, when Murray didn't show up to spend any time with her and her children, she made the decision to take matters into her own hands. Bundy attempted to bribe Jeanette into leaving her husband – which Jeanette accepted, as long as this was Murray's desire, as well. Bundy left with the hope that later that evening, she and Murray would finally be able to start their life together. But when Murray came to talk to her after discussing the situation with his wife, he told Bundy to "stay out of his life," telling her there was "no way" he would let her break up his family.

Devastated, Bundy spent a few days licking her wounds, but still turned up three days later at Murray's favorite bar, the "Little Nashville Club." Murray regularly played music at the bar, but that night, he was simply enjoying himself off-stage, dancing with his wife. Heartbroken, Bundy felt her dream of a life with Murray slip further and further away – but caught the eye of an attractive blond gentleman, who she saw watching her from across the bar.

After an evening of dancing, Bundy was taken with the stranger from the bar. Rather than taking advantage of her promiscuity, this new man treated Bundy with respect – which made her feel like a true lady, cherished and appreciated. Charmed, Bundy felt like she and Doug Clark were made for each other, and was already looking forward to seeing him again when he dropped her off at home and promised to call on her soon.

A whirlwind romance

Doug Clark waited only a few days before calling Bundy and asking to see her again. Although Bundy preferred to keep her male callers away from her children, she relented when Clark suggested he come over for dinner – and was pleased to see that her boys took to him immediately. They played, cuddled, and Clark even tucked the boys in for bed before telling them that he would be spending the night with their mother. Bundy loved the way he took care of things, and was more than willing to give him complete control.

For the first time, Bundy made love with a partner who seemed truly interested in giving her pleasure, rather than just letting her do all the work. He was an affectionate lover, telling her over and over again how much he wanted her, how much he appreciated her, how smart and beautiful she was. This was all new to Bundy, and played right into her desperate need for validation.

The next morning, however, Bundy awoke to see Clark looking concerned and anxious – his landlady was causing him grief, he said, so would she mind terribly if he moved some of his things into her apartment? Enamoured, Bundy was eager to accommodate Clark's desires, even when he requested a pair of her panties – just so he could remember her, even when they were apart. Although she felt somewhat uncomfortable with it, Bundy gave her new lover a pair of her large, cotton panties, which he promptly returned to her when he saw how big they were. Bundy was hurt, but she was still thrilled to have found such an attractive, caring, respectful man who was so interested in her.

Still, Clark's attentions weren't enough to tear Bundy away from Murray. After sending him several letters professing her deep, unwavering love for him, Bundy made another attempt to manipulate him away from his wife. This time, though, Murray refused to indulge Bundy's long-standing delusions, and told her it was finally time to move out of the building. Although reluctant, Bundy moved into a new apartment just three miles away – big enough for herself, her two sons, and her new lover.

After moving her furniture into the new suite, Murray left with his wife, but returned frequently to have sex with Bundy or persuade her into lending him more money. Not surprisingly, Murray and Clark disliked each other immediately, which Bundy interpreted as jealousy – a sign of their love for her. She told Clark how Murray had exploited her affection for him by asking for loans and gifts. Enraged, Clark demanded that Bundy cut him off immediately. She agreed, but kept the joint account open.

The perfect couple

Clark's anger over Murray's mistreatment of Bundy encouraged her enough to overlook the fact that her new live-in boyfriend wasn't covering his share of the rent, bills, or food. Bundy's new job at Valley Medical Centre, where she was now working as a vocational nurse, paid her more than enough to cover the expenses – and Bundy was content to take care of everything, as long as Clark continued to provide her with his love and affection.

Unfortunately, Clark was having a hard time keeping this up. He was proving himself to be just as self-absorbed as Murray – talking constantly about himself and his needs, with no real interest in hearing about anything Bundy brought up. However, the couple grew closer together after Clark read an article about expressing true love by fulfilling each other's fantasies. Eagerly, Clark convinced Bundy to start opening up about her own sexual desires, and he began to do the same.

Clark's fantasies were dark, but Bundy was thrilled that he was sharing these intimate thoughts with her. Bundy had a budding interest in bondage and domination, and particularly enjoyed imagining herself as Clark's captured sex slave – although in his fantasy, this role was filled by some young girl. But Clark loved that Bundy's sexual limits seemed virtually non-existent, and he pushed to include even darker subject matter, even murder. If she loved him, Clark told Bundy, she "should be willing to kill for him." Desperate to please him, she assured him that she would.

Their relationship was inconsistent. Clark would regularly disappear for hours and even days at a time, withdrawing from Bundy and drawing out her deepest insecurities. When he would eventually return, Bundy would be so relieved and happy to see him that she would say anything to convince him to stay. She also continued to react with pleasure and excitement as Clark's nighttime fantasy sharing grew increasingly sordid and graphic – even when he told her details of an ex-girlfriend's experiences with necrophilia.

A near escape

Bundy's penchant for promiscuity led her to browse personal ads occasionally, especially during Clark's frequent absences. When a posting from a well-to-do studio executive named Art Pollinger caught her eye, Bundy bravely responded to the ad. Pollinger weighed nearly four hundred pounds, but he was looking for a wife and thought Bundy a worthy prospect. Her tried-and-true method of using her past abuses to entice new lovers paid off again, and Pollinger – who genuinely enjoyed Bundy's company and thought her to be an intelligent and interesting woman – encouraged her to cut ties with Murray.

Eventually, after some persuading, Bundy allowed Polliger to drive her to the bank, where she withdrew the money she had left in the joint safety-deposit box she'd opened with Murray. Nearly $6000 was missing, and withdrawal slips were signed with Murray's name, but Bundy continued to defend Murray's deceit. Still, she took the rest of the money and put it in a chequing account where Murray would be unable to access it.

Despite Pollinger's genuine affection and desire to share his life with Bundy, the two ended up parting ways. Bundy was used to the emotional abuse she had endured in her previous relationships, and couldn't be satisfied in a healthy relationship.

Red flags

After having surgery to restore her sight, Bundy was excited at the prospect of purchasing a new car – and so was Clark, who had selected a blue 1973 Buick station wagon. Even though the car was large and difficult for Bundy to drive, since her peripheral vision was severely limited, she bought it anyway. She was desperate to give Clark everything he asked for – even guns, which he said she should have for protection. From a pawn shop in Van Nuys, Clark selected two .25 calibre Raven automatics, which Bundy was more than willing to pay for and register in her own name.

By now, Bundy's older son was starting to notice how Clark dominated his mother, and begged her to kick him out. Instead of taking her child's concern to heart, however, Bundy refused to acknowledge Clark's abuse – choosing to lash out at her son, instead. Clark and Bundy regularly beat him, and once, Clark even graphically detailed how he could kill the boy – with Bundy's son right next to him. Rather than defending her child, though, Bundy merely watched as Clark's behaviour grew more and more violent.

The couple had even stopped having sex, as Clark informed Bundy that she was too unattractive to arouse him anymore. Desperate to please him, Bundy began accompanying Clark as he picked up prostitutes from the Sunset Strip, and would watch from the backseat while he forced the usually young women to service him orally.

According to former FBI Special Agent Robert R. Hazelwood, who worked with the Behavioural Sciences Unit, men like Clark employ a specific process that can turn vulnerable women into accomplices. After identifying a woman like Bundy, desperate for attention, they use seduction techniques to reshape the woman's sexual norms – even if the woman is initially disturbed or frightened.

"These men have the ability to recognize vulnerable women and manipulate them," Hazelwood said. "The behaviour gets reinforced with attention and affection, gifts and excitement. Eventually, they are doing things that isolate them and further lower their self-esteem. All they have is this guy, so they cooperate."

Clark had plenty of experience in charming women enough to get them to do whatever he wanted, but although he had tried, he had been unable to find a suitable woman to replace Bundy. None of the other women he dated were as willing to indulge his dark sexual fantasies as Bundy was, so despite his mounting contempt for her, Clark continued to live with Bundy on and off. Bundy reassured herself that even though Clark had other girlfriends, she was the one he shared his intimate fantasies with – his feelings for her, she thought, must be deeper.

More than just fantasies

When Clark showed up at her apartment in late April, 1980, covered in blood, Bundy realized his murderous tendencies had taken a step beyond his imagination. Although Bundy chose to believe a fabricated tale Clark wove where he'd been attacked by a girl's boyfriend, the real story came out when a young prostitute named Charlene identified Doug Clark as the man who had stabbed her repeatedly with a knife after picking her up and requesting oral sex. She had been lucky to escape alive.

Bundy's suspicions mounted further when she discovered a bag of clothes and a blanket in the backseat of the Buick – covered in blood. When she confronted Clark, he told her the same kind of graphic story of sexual perversion that she'd become accustomed to hearing – only this time, the story was real.

Clark had spotted two young runaways, 15-year-old Cindy and her 16-year-old stepsister, Gina, at a bus stop. After picking them up and demanding Cindy give him oral sex, he told Bundy that he shot both girls until they were dead and then drove with the bodies to a garage he rented in Burbank. Once inside the garage, Clark said he dragged the bodies onto an old mattress and proceeded to perform acts of necrophilia on their corpses.

That night, after confessing to Bundy, Clark returned to the garage with a camera borrowed from one of his other girlfriends. After playing with the bodies again, he wrapped them in the blanket and dumped them in a ditch off the Ventura Freeway. Bundy was thrilled that he'd chosen to confess this activity to her, instead of any of the other women he was involved with.

Still, Bundy felt compelled to report the murders to the Van Nuys police. When she called the department the night after Clark's confession, she told the officer that she believed her boyfriend had committed the crime. Although Bundy told the officer some details of the case, she wasn't taken seriously, and when the call was disconnected, they assumed the "crank caller" had just hung up.

Clark started telling Bundy about other murders he claimed to have committed, including the killing of a man named Vic Weiss and the slaying of a young prostitute identified by police as teenage runaway Marnett Comer. Their relationship had become completely centered around Clark's murderous desires and Bundy's desperate need for his attention. Even though he no longer made any attempt to flatter or even be kind to Bundy, Clark had her completely under his control.

Only a few months later, at the end of June, Bundy accompanied Clark on what would be their first murder together. Cathy, who the couple picked up off Hollywood's Highland Avenue, looked about 17 years old, and agreed to perform oral sex on Clark for $30. Bundy, watching from the backseat, passed Clark the gun when Cathy failed to get him erect. He shot her, and as she lay dying with her head in Bundy's lap, Clark drove the car out into the country. Cathy was left along a gravel road near the Magic Mountain amusement park.

The very next night, Clark came home and told Bundy of another killing. He'd spotted three prostitutes working together, and convinced one of them, Exxie Wilson, to get in the Buick. After killing her and cutting off her head, Clark realized the other two women might be able to identify him if Wilson's body was found, so he went back and picked up one of the other prostitutes, later identified as Karen Jones. Clark left Jones' body near the Burbank Studios, and, after giving up on finding the third girl, returned to Bundy's apartment with Wilson's head.

They kept the head in the freezer for a few days, and Clark told Bundy how he would take it into the shower with him and push his penis into the open mouth. Eventually, Bundy cleaned the head and put it in an ornate treasure chest, which they dumped near the Studio City Sizzler where Clark had left the rest of Wilson's body. The chest was discovered almost immediately, and the relationship between Bundy and Clark grew even more strained.

The unraveling

In an attempt to gain back Clark's affections, Bundy agreed to participate in a three-way sexual relationship involving their 11-year-old neighbour, who Clark had been molesting for months. Since news of the Sunset Strip murders was spreading, prostitutes were hesitant to work alone, and it was increasingly difficult for Clark and Bundy to find anyone willing to get in their car.

Police were holding press conferences where they discussed evidence that seemed to link the cases – leading them to believe this may be the work of a serial killer. It was even suspected that the killer lived in the area, Detective Sergeant John Helvin stated to the press, "but we don't know for sure."

The stress of this ongoing investigation and Clark's lack of interest in her led Bundy to a desperate suicide attempt, and when she woke up alone at a hospital in Burbank, Bundy called Murray to come pick her up.

Bundy was willing to do anything to reignite Murray's sexual interest in her, so she started bringing her young neighbour for him to fondle. When that still wasn't enough, Bundy turned to her reliable method of playing the victim to gain her lover's sympathy – she told Murray about the murders. Although Murray didn't threaten to tell the police, Bundy knew she couldn't keep him alive. Besides, this was her opportunity to prove to Clark that she would kill for him.

On August 3, 1980, Murray climbed into the back of his van, anticipating oral sex. Instead, Bundy shot him in the head twice and stabbed him in the back half a dozen times. When she realized the bullets in Murray's head would help the police identify her gun, she cut his head off and put it in a plastic bag, eventually dumping it in a trash can near Griffith Park.

The rest of his body was found just days later, left in his van in the parking lot at the Little Nashville club. Police began questioning regulars at the club, including Murray's wife, Jeanette. Bundy was brought down to the police station dand gave detectives her version of the alibi she had already discussed with Clark, which included a detailed description of a man she had supposedly sold her two guns to.

But none of this was enough for Clark, who refused to accept any of the blame for the rapidly deteriorating situation. He told Bundy that he was moving out, and left her alone while he went out to spend time with a new girlfriend. After briefly speaking to her mother-in-law and her sons, Bundy called Geis and told him about the murders. The next morning, after being berated by Clark as she drove him to work, Bundy confessed to a co-worker about the crime spree. By the end of the day, both Clark and Bundy were arrested in relation to the series of Sunset Strip murders.

According to police commander William Booth, evidence gathered during the investigation of Murray's death, along with the information collected during the ongoing investigation into the Sunset Strip murders, let them to Clark and Bundy. Bundy would end up telling the police graphic details about each murder, admitting that she thought killing was "really fun to do."

The end of the Sunset Strip

Despite the mountains of evidence connecting Clark to the killings, he continued to claim his innocence – even after he was found guilty on six counts of murder and sentenced to death. Bundy, who had initially entered a plea of "not guilty by reason of insanity," managed to avoid a similar fate by pleading guilty to her two counts of murder. She was sentenced to two consecutive terms of 25 years to life, with an added two years for using a firearm illegally.

Until her death in 2003, Bundy fought desperately to prove Clark's innocence – even as he attempted to put all the blame on her.

A COUPLE THAT KILLS

KARL BRIGHTSON

James Marlow and Cynthia Coffman were a troubled couple who were convicted of murdering five people during a deadly rampage that spanned multiple states. The last two victims, 20-year old Corrina Novis and 19-year old Lynell Murray were kidnapped and found strangled and sodomized, and the murderous pair were found guilty of the crimes. Whereas both Marlow and Coffman received the death penalty for Novis' death, Marlow received a second death sentence for Murray's while Coffman was sentence to life without the possibility of parole in Murray's murder. Both defendants sought to shift the onus of blame to the other with Marlow claiming it was Coffman's idea to kill the girls while he only wanted to rob them and Coffman alleging that she was the victim of battered women's syndrome. Neither ploy was successful as the pair were convicted across the board for robbery, kidnapping, sodomy, and murder. Coffman has the distinction of being the first woman sentenced to death in California following the state's reinstatement of the death penalty in 1977.

Early Lives

James

James Gregory Marlow was born on 11 May 1956 in Ohio but raised in Kentucky; the son of a beautiful but amoral hillbilly woman named Doris who virtually ensured that her son would grow up completely dysfunctional. Throughout his childhood, Marlow witnessed abuse, neglect, drug use, and sex courtesy of his mother who often prostituted herself in front of him. She gave birth to another child, Veronica Koppers, in 1959 and would frequently leave her children alone or with neighbors. Marlow eventually went to live with his father, Arnold, who would beat him severely and lock him in cabinets and, subsequently, went back to his mother's house. Despite the abuse and her horrific behavior, Marlow loved his mother dearly.

So much, in fact, that when he was 13 years old his mother shot him up with drugs and seduced him. During interviews Marlow openly admitted to having had sexual relations with his mother on several occasions and that he didn't know it was wrong. He loved his mother so much and thought it was normal. Experts assert that Marlow suffered from traumatic bonding in which a traumatic event—his mother's seduction—created a dysfunctional yet significant bond from which he could not escape.

By the time Marlow was 16 years old he was living alone in California and married his first of three wives. Thanks to his mother, Marlow developed a severely skewed view of women. When she died in a trailer fire he was completely distraught and "took on the sins of his parents" by turning to a life of crime and violence. In one incident when he was still a teenager, Marlow was talking to one of his cousin's girlfriend, Darlene Miller, who he—one day while driving her to a nearby convenience store—pulled over in front of an old, abandoned house and forced Miller into the house where he beat and hogtied her, and then locked her in a closet. Over a span of three days Marlow would repeatedly beat, rape, and sodomize Miller. She escaped and ran to a neighbor's house—a house that Marlow had recently burglarized. Police were called and Marlow was arrested and after a tearful pretrial interview wherein he tearfully detailed the issues with his mother, he was sent to a drug rehabilitation center in 1975 for seven months and, soon after his release in 1976 was rearrested for being under the influence. Marlow was eventually imprisoned for burglary, robbery, and drug charges and was ultimately sentenced to California's notorious Folsom Prison in 1980. It was here that Marlow—not unlike the majority of inmates—got heavily tattooed with one—a howling wolf on his right side—earning him the nickname of the Folsom Wolf.

Prior to meeting Coffman, Marlow had an extensive criminal record. On 5 November 1979 in Upland, California, Marlow and his friend Allen Smallwood, who were both heroin addicts, assaulted

Jeffrey Johnson in his apartment, searched it for non-existent drugs, then took Johnson downstairs—by knifepoint—to the Liesches' apartment where they searched the second apartment for more non-existent drugs, tied up the residents—Lori and Kathy—with electrical cords, and stole some cash they had found.

The following day, Marlow entered an Upland, California, leather goods store owned by Joanne Gilligan who was helping a customer, said he had a gun in his pocket and ordered them to lie on the floor, and then robbed the register of cash and took two jackets.

At approximately 10:00 a.m. on 20 November that same year, Gertrude Smith and Wilson Lee were working at an Ontario, California, methadone clinic when Marlow and Smallwood entered brandishing a sawed-off shotgun and pistol, respectively, and demanded methadone which they were told was locked in a safe. Another employee opened the safe and the two left with methadone that had a street value of $10,000. When Marlow was finally arrested on 26 November he had a bottle of methadone in his jacket and had the shotgun wrapped in a shirt.

Cynthia

Cynthia Lynn Haskins was born on 19 January 1962 in St. Louis, Missouri. From the beginning her life was to be difficult. Born with a double hernia that precluded her mother from holding her, Cynthia never experienced the necessary mother-infant bonding so crucial for healthy adjustment. As a result, she suffered from a crucial lack of empathy and a driving propensity to seek affections elsewhere. Cynthia's father left when she was three years old and her mother—who had aspirations of becoming a singer—allegedly tried to give her and her brothers Robbie and Jeff away several times during their childhood; with Jeff eventually given up for adoption. Cynthia was frequently "farmed out" to relatives that made her become more rebellious, defiant, and reckless. By the time she was a sophomore in high school, Cynthia was already experimenting with marijuana and methamphetamine with her new friends.

Her mother remarried a successful businessman named Bill Maender with whom Cynthia did not get along. Truancy, rebelliousness, and ultimately not wanting to live by her stepfather's rules caused Cynthia to run away at age 17 to her boyfriend's, Ron Coffman, house. When Cynthia returned three months later, pregnant, abortion was not an option for her devout parents and she refused to give the baby up for adoption, so she was forced into a loveless marriage with Coffman. The marriage quickly deteriorated and Ron filed for divorce because of Cynthia's infidelities, drug use, and poor housekeeping while Cynthia accused him of physical and emotional abuse and infidelity. Cynthia then worked in a carburetor factory to take care of her son, Joshua. She ultimately abandoned Joshua after two years, leaving him with her ex-husband (allegedly intending to get him back after she got settled) although later, when she and Marlow were committing their heinous crimes she suggested that Marlow kill her ex-husband and ex-in-laws (who had legal custody of Joshua) so she could regain custody of her son. While on death row Coffman exchanges letters with her son who believes his mother to be in prison for drug-related charges. She has stated in interviews that she wants to be the one to tell him the truth someday.

There is much speculation that Coffman had antisocial personality disorder which is characterized by little regard for right and wrong or the feelings of others. Further, those with the chronic disorder tend to manipulate, antagonize, and treat others with a callous indifference, are very prone to violate the law, are easily angered, lie, behave impulsively and/or violently, and use and abuse drugs and alcohol—all without remorse or guilt. Coffman exhibited a number of these traits, many of which worsened once she began her relationship with Marlow.

In May 1984 Coffman left home with a girlfriend and journeyed west where she wound up in Page, Arizona, and moved in with her new boyfriend, Doug Huntley. The lovebirds moved to Barstow, California where Huntley had some friends. He secured employment in construction while she was a bartender and waitress and sold methamphetamines on the side. One evening they were involved in an altercation outside of a convenience store in which Coffman pulled a gun on several men who were hassling her boyfriend and this resulted in both Huntley and Coffman being arrested and jailed. While Coffman was released after a few days, Huntley became cellmates with Marlow. Huntley told Marlow all about Coffman which intrigued Marlow who, upon his release soon thereafter, showed up at Coffman's apartment. It was love at first sight as Coffman reminded Marlow of his mother and Marlow was every bit the bad boy to whom Coffman was attracted. Even after Huntley was released, Marlow, Coffman, and he remained friends until Huntley returned to prison in June of that year.

A Dangerous Partnership

Marlow and Coffman began their contentious, dysfunctional, and murderous relationship amidst drugs and violence; her former boyfriend Huntley all but forgotten. In June 1986 Marlow had Coffman drive him to Fontana, California, and to his cousin Debbie Schwab's house where he purchased methamphetamines. A few days later they went to Newberry Springs and stayed with some of Marlow's friends, Steve and Karen Schmitt. Marlow told Coffman that he was a hit man, a martial arts expert, and a White supremacist who had murdered African American while in prison. It was during this time that Coffman saw Marlow turn into "Wolf"—his angry, violent alter-ego. Coffman testified in court that Marlow would beat her and then apologize and things would be fine again for a while. This is classic cycle-of-violence behavior central to most domestic violence cases. At this point Marlow allegedly took Coffman's address book that had her mother's and son's addresses and refused to give it back to her; essentially holding it as a carrot just out of reach to get her to do what he wanted.

They traveled across the country visiting Marlow's relatives in Kentucky and Tennessee. He had told Marlow that his father had recently died and left him some land in Kentucky and that they could get her son and live as a family there. First, however, they needed a vehicle and Marlow allegedly pressured Coffman to steal her friend's red Nissan pickup truck that Marlow and friend Paul Donner painted black. Marlow and Coffman jumped in the truck, stole some license plates from an off road vehicle outside of Newberry Springs, California, and headed east.

In Woodland Park, Colorado, Marlow called Gene Kelly, a contractor who constructed microwave telephone relay towers and who Marlow had met when he was a temporary laborer for him a few years back, to see if he needed any help in Colorado at the time. (There is some discrepancy in the available literature with respect to this individual being named Gene Kelly or Elmer Lutz; however, the actual criminal case against the defendants state Kelly). Kelly told him that he didn't have any work at the time but that he would have some work in Atlanta, Georgia, in a few weeks. The couple went to Colorado Springs for a couple of days and then to St. Louis to see Coffman's grandmother. They arrived on 2 July and Coffman called her mother who was less than happy to hear from her. The couple continued their journey east.

In Pine Knot, Kentucky, Marlow called his cousin Donald "Lardo" Lyons and both he and Coffman stayed with him for several days. Marlow had expected a modest inheritance from his grandmother Lena Walls with whom Marlow and his sister Veronica were close when they were younger; however, by the time Marlow reached Kentucky there was nothing left for him. Needing money, Marlow agreed to meet with Lardo's friend Shannon "Killer" Compton and the trio discussed how a local man named Greg "Wildman" Hill was going to be testifying in court against a mutual acquaintance and that Hill should "be silenced." They arranged for Compton to give Lyons a sum of money of which Lyons would give $5,000 to Marlow to get rid of Hill.

The next day, 7 July 1986, Lyons gave Marlow a .22 caliber pistol and at 5:00 a.m. Marlow and Coffman got into their stolen black Nissan pickup and drove to Hill's house. For most of the day the two of them parked relatively close and surveilled his house, did drugs, and engaged in sex. Finally, Marlow ordered Coffman to take off her shirt and bra and to tie a bandana across her chest like a bikini top and to knock on Hill's door to elicit help for her "stalled" truck. Hill agreed and tucked his own pistol inside his jeans' waistband. At the truck, when Marlow came after Hill with his own gun, Hill drew his and after an ensuing struggle Hill's gun went off, mortally wounding him with a bullet to the head. Marlow wiped his fingerprints off Hill's gun and left it at the scene.

Lyons kept true to his word giving Marlow the $5,000 "fee" for his "hit." The next day Marlow gave the stolen Nissan to a relative and spent $3,000 on a Harley Davidson; something he wanted for a very long time. On 11 July 1986 Marlow and Coffman had a "biker" wedding atop a Marlow's new Harley. Witnesses alleged that Coffman's face was bruised and scratched from a recent beating Marlow have given her. Such violence was not an isolated incident. In fact, one time while Marlow was assaulting Coffman one of his acquaintances asked what he was doing and Marlow dislocated his arm. As a result, nobody else ever intervened when Marlow was in one of his rages against Coffman. She said that when Marlow turns into "Wolf" his voice becomes monotone and his eyes and facial expression changes—that he becomes a completely different and violent person.

Marlow ended up giving the Nissan to a friend and purchasing a 1970's Cadillac to continue their journey to Atlanta and a job with Kelly. Marlow did manage to work for four days before an incident wherein he, Coffman, and a group of coworkers went out for dinner but which turned into Marlow beating Coffman outside of the restaurant and inside the vehicle, seemingly because she assisted some men with a stuck ball at a pool table. Back at the hotel where they were staying, Marlow was not finished with Coffman. He asked her for her scissors and then queried, "Your hair or your eye?" Horrified, Coffman said her hair and Marlow cut it as short as he could with her small scissors. He then taunted her that he would pierce her eye as well before making her strip naked and forcing her to stand outside the hotel room for several minutes. He then let her back into the room where he forcibly sodomized her. The following morning Marlow found a check from Kelly that had been slid under the door for his four days of work. After a few more days of going on "pot hunts" and unsuccessfully attempting a burglary in July 1986 in Whitley County, Kentucky, the couple left and headed back to Arizona.

In Arizona, Marlow and Coffman burglarized her former boyfriend Doug Huntley's parents' house and stole their safe that contained ten silver dollars—which they kept—and some papers. They buried the safe in the dessert. The next stop was back in Newberry Springs, California, where the couple stole two rings from the Schmitts; one they pawned for cash and the other they traded for methamphetamines.

Returning to Fontana, California, in early October 1986, Marlow and Coffman stayed with his cousins, the Schwabs. During their visit Marlow tattooed "Property of Folsom Wolf" on Coffman's buttocks and the word "W-O-L-F" and some lightning bolts on her ring finger as a wedding band. They then spent some time with Marlow's friends Rita Robbeloth and her son Curtis, and then with his sister, her husband Paul Koppers, and his brother, Steve. During this time Coffman alleges that after asking for an equal share of the methamphetamine they had, Marlow became angry and beat her, threatened to kill her, forced her to consume pills he said were cyanide, extinguished a cigarette on her face, and stabbed her in the leg. The pair then went to stay with another of Marlow's friends, Richard Drinkhouse.

The Crimes

On 11 October 1986 they were linked to the death of 32-year old Sandra Neary of Costa Mesa, California who never returned from a quick trip to a local ATM machine to withdraw some money. Her car was found in a nearby parking lot and her body was later found on 24 October by some hikers near Corona, California. Their next victim was 35-year old Pamela Simmons. She was reported missing in Bullhead City, Arizona, on 28 October. Her abandoned car was found by the local police department and the theory was that she was also abducted while withdrawing money from an ATM.

Corinna Novis

On 7 November, 20-year old Corinna Novis vanished from a First Interstate Bank parking lot near a shopping mall in Redlands, California, in broad daylight. Alone, she was driving her white Honda CR-X and when she failed to make her manicure appointment at her friend Terry Davis' salon, and then failed to make a 7:00 p.m. pizza date with other friends, she was reported missing. That same day, Marlow and Coffman were at the Redlands Mall visiting his sister Koppers who worked at a restaurant and were supposed to pick her up from work; however, Marlow gave his sister back her keys, telling her that they already had a ride. Coffman, clad in a dress, and Marlow, in a suit and tie, probably seemed rather innocuous to Novis when they asked her for a ride. Earlier that day Marlow had told Coffman that they needed to "get a girl" but Coffman alleged that she did not know that Marlow intended to kill her.

At approximately 7:30 p.m., they took Novis to Marlow's friend Richard Drinkhouse's house who was home alone recovering from a motorcycle accident at the time. Coffman took their hostage into the bedroom after telling Drinkhouse they needed to use the bathroom. Marlow told Drinkhouse that Coffman was trying to get her ATM pin number so they could "rob" her bank account. Drinkhouse didn't appreciate their intrusion into his house to which Marlow assured Drinkhouse that that there wouldn't be any witnesses because how could Novis talk to anyone "if she's under a pile of rocks"? Soon thereafter, Marlow's sister Koppers showed up and she and Coffman left the house to go to a nearby 7-Eleven while Marlow cautioned Drinkhouse not to leave and then returned to the bedroom where Novis was. After Coffman returned, she went into the bedroom to change clothes and after what sounded like the shower running the three of them emerged from the bedroom—Novis' and Marlow's hair were wet (Coffman testified that she had nothing to do with "what went on in the shower"). Novis was handcuffed and had duct tape over her mouth. They left the house and Drinkhouse testified that he never saw Novis again.

The next day, Marlow and Coffman asked Drinkhouse if he wanted to buy an answering machine. Novis' employer Jean Cramer, went to check on her the morning of 10 November when she uncharacteristically failed to appear at work and didn't call. She noticed Novis' car was missing, her front door was ajar, and her bedroom was in disarray. There was no evidence of forced entry and Novis' typewriter and answering machine were missing. On 7 November Koppers sold Novis' answering machine to a friend in exchange for a half-gram of methamphetamine who sold it to someone else and the Redlands Police Department ultimately recovered it. The next day, Harold Brigham who owned the Sierra Jewelry and Loan in Fontana testified that Coffman pawned Novis' typewriter using the victim's identification.

Back at the Robbeloths' house Coffman said Marlow changed clothes and tried to access money from Novis' account at a local First Interstate Bank; however, the PIN number she gave them was incorrect. The following day they ransacked Novis' apartment, found her PIN number, stole her money, pawned the typewriter they stole, disposed of Novis' belongings and then returned to Drinkhouse's house. On 12 November Marlow found out that his sister was in police custody and he and Coffman drove to Big Bear to get rid of Novis' car. They checked into the Bavarian Lodge using a credit card from another victim, Lynell Murray. They abandoned Novis' car on a dirt road south of Santa's Village which was approximately a quarter mile off of Highway 18 in the area. Coffman's fingerprints were found on the license plate, hood, and ashtray while Marlow's prints were found on the hood. The two then proceeded to walk along Big Bear Boulevard clad only in bathing suits despite the chilly weather; the stolen clothes that they had been wearing were discarded along with the handcuffs used on Novis. Receipts for clothing purchased by Marlow and Coffman were found in the clothing's pockets. The .22 caliber pistol the couple owned was in Coffman's purse.

Novis' body was discovered on 15 November lying face down in a shallow grave at a Fontana vineyard. She had been strangled and sodomized.

Dr. Gregory Reiber performed Novis' autopsy on 17 November and conclude that time of death was between five and ten days prior. Evidence of marks on her neck, injuries to her neck muscles, and thyroid cartilage fracture suggested death by strangulation; however, the presence of dirt in her throat also suggested possible suffocation. There was also biological evidence of sodomy.

Lynell Murray

On 12 November, 19-year old psychology student and Prime Cleaners dry cleaning shop clerk Lynell Murray failed to keep a date with her boyfriend, Robert Whitecotton, in Orange County. After noticing that the cleaners looked as though it had been burglarized and ransacked and that Murray's car was parked in the parking lot out back he called the police.

Murray had no idea that the previous day Marlow and Coffman saw her leaving work and that Marlow had commented that she would be "a good one to rob." The following evening at approximately 6:00 p.m., shortly before Murray was to leave work, one Lynda Schafer entered the cleaners and dropped of some clothes with Murray. Schafer would later testify that she saw Coffman "passionately embracing a man", later identified as Marlow, in an alley behind the cleaners.

At 6:30 p.m. that evening Coffman approached Linda Whitlake who was leaving her gym and asked for a ride to her motel, claiming that her car wouldn't start. After Whitlake noticed Marlow in Novis' white car with its hood up she changed her mind about giving them a ride. Coffman said that her boyfriend had decided to call the auto club instead and Whitlake left.

At 7:13 p.m. Coffman checked into room 307 of the Huntington Beach Inn under the name Lynell Murray and used Murray's credit card. At 8:19 p.m. a Bank of America branch in Corona del Mar recorded a balance inquiry into Murray's account and a subsequent withdrawal of $80 occurred, shortly followed by a $60 withdrawal, which left a balance of $4.41. Later that evening Coffman checked into the Compri Hotel in Ontario, California, with Murray's credit card. At midnight Marlow and Coffman ate dinner at the Denny's restaurant across from the hotel, which they paid for with Murray's credit card.

Murray's body would be discovered the following day at approximately 3:00 p.m. in room 307 at the Huntington Beach Inn. Her head was in the bathtub in six inches of water with it and her face bound with strips of towel. She was gagged. Her right arm was secured to her waist with a towel. Her right leg was atop the toilet and her left leg was on the floor. Her ankles looked to have been bound with duct tape as residue was evident. Her bra, nylons, and one earring were missing and she looked to have been raped and urinated on. She had also suffered pre-mortem blunt force trauma to the head, torso injuries, two black eyes, and leg bruising which were consistent with being beaten. The cause of death was determined to be ligature strangulation.

Police finally turned their attention to Marlow and Coffman after finding Novis' driver's license and checkbook in a Taco Bell takeout bag near a dumpster in Laguna Niguel along with papers with both Marlow's and Coffman's names on them. Marlow had attempted to dispose of this damning evidence but missed the dumpster. A statewide alert was issued for both Marlow and Coffman.

Arrest

On 14 November, police were dispatched to a Big Bear, California, mountain lodge after being alerted that Murray's credit card was being used to purchase clothes at a local sporting goods store. The owner of the lodge identified Marlow and Coffman as his latest guests. After finding the lodge empty, the 100-man posse discovered the suspects walking along a mountain road at approximately 3:00 p.m. They surrendered without incident, clad in clothing they had stolen from the dry cleaning shop where Murray had worked. A few hours later Coffman led police to Novis' body. One of the victim's earrings, a .22 caliber pistol and ammunition, credit card receipts with Murray's forged signature, and a Prime Cleaners paper bag with coins were found in Coffman's purse.

The Trial

Nearly three years later Marlow and Coffman would stand trial which commenced on 18 July 1989 in San Bernardino County. At several points throughout the proceedings motions for severance filed by both defendants were denied.

Among the overwhelming evidence were both defendants' fingerprints in Novis' car and that, as previously mentioned, Coffman was linked to the Fontana pawn shop where Novis' typewriter was pawned. In room 307 of the Huntington Beach Inn where Lynell Murray's body was found, a footprint on a bathmat by her body was consistent with Marlow's boots. The aforementioned Taco Bell bag with Novis' license and checkbook and documentation with Coffman's and Marlow's names was recovered. Credit card activity demonstrated where and when the defendants had used Murray's credit card. Additionally, the discarded suit jacket that Marlow had worn when they abducted Novis was found at the Bavarian Lodge and contained identification bearing Marlow's name, various single earrings presumed to be trophies from the murders, a blue ladies wallet, and the handcuffs used on Novis. Novis' vehicle was found near Santa's Village with license plates stolen from a vehicle that was at the Huntington Beach Inn and in a nearby trash can a maintenance worker found a pillowcase containing Murray's bra and laundry receipts from the cleaners where Murray had worked.

Coffman took the stand in her own behalf, painting Marlow to be an abusive man who was violent toward her and threatened both her and her son. She alleged that any violence directed toward the victims were perpetrated by Marlow. With respect to Novis, Coffman testified that on the night of Novis' death, she had dropped Novis and Marlow off at the vineyard and was told to go purchase methamphetamines. Coffman alleges that she drove a short distance, stopped and smoked a cigarette, and then returned to "the sound of digging." Marlow returned to the vehicle alone, threw some items in the back of the car, and then started to beat her for driving away.

Coffman's attorney presented numerous witnesses who corroborated Coffman's allegations of Marlow's violence including Katherine Davis, one of Marlow's ex-wives, and her mother Marlene Boggs; Coffman's former employers in Arizona; Coffman's mother Carol Maender; and clinical psychologist Craig Rath who claimed that Coffman's relationship with Marlow was "precipitated by impaired bonding in her early life", that she was not malingering, and that she did not suffer from antisocial personality disorder.

In Marlow's defense, his sister Veronica Koppers testified about the abuse and neglect the two suffered at the hands of their mother and her father Wendell Hill; about how her father shot her mother and her mother stabbed her father seven times which prompted Doris to move to California in 1963; about visiting her mother at the Sybil Brand Institute for Women and the Frontera State Prison; about how Doris introduced her daughter to drugs much like she did with Marlow and taught her how to burglarize houses; and about the myriad drinking and drug parties hosted at their house. Several witnesses at the trial testified that Doris rarely even mentioned that she had children and paid them little attention when they were together. Despite Marlow claiming responsibility for the murder in Kentucky as well as Novis' and Murray's in California he tried to shift the majority of blame onto Coffman much as she attempted to do to him.

Throughout the trial, Coffman's legal team tried to utilize the "Patty Hearst" defense that she was brainwashed, starved, and the victim of battered women's syndrome who was subjected to frequent physical, emotional, and mental abuse. Once, she claimed, Marlow beat her with a motorcycle clutch plate bruising her face and another time kicked her with his steel-toed boots. She stated that she feared for both her life and that of her then-six-year old son. Coffman's side even presented an expert on battered women's syndrome; however, the jury apparently rejected such claims.

Other testimony suggested that Coffman was the true ringleader and cold, calculated murderess, being far more intelligent than Marlow who would do anything to keep her. At one point, prosecutor Robert Gannon asked Coffman whether her relationship with Marlow was more important than the lives of Corinna Novis and Lynell Murray to which she replied, "Yes."

Sentencing

Both defendants were convicted of the kidnapping, robbery, kidnapping for robbery, residential burglary, forcible sodomy, and murder of Novis and subsequently sentenced to death on 30 August 1989. Coffman became the first women sentenced to death in

California since the state reinstated capital punishment in 1977; however, California's reputation as an overly liberal state makes it unlikely that Coffman will ever be put to death.

On 8 March 1992 Marlow received a second death sentence for Murray's murder while Coffman received a life without the possibility of parole sentence added to her death sentence, the former rather moot.

On 19 August 2004 the California Supreme Court unanimously upheld both Marlow's and Coffman's death sentences.

Post-conviction

There continues to be speculation as to whether Coffman controlled or was controlled by Marlow. In fact, while on Death Row, Marlow wrote *I Wish You Were Never Born*, a novel detailing Coffman's and his murderous spree (proceeds of the sale of his book are donated to help abused children). He asserts that their story in the popular media—including an episode of *Wicked Attractions*—was sensationalized and he wanted the truth to be known.

COLD BLOODED CHARMER : SERIAL KILLER SHAWN GRATE

87

JESSE DIXON

A desperate plea for help

On September 13, 2016, a call came through Ashland, Ohio's 911 system from a distressed woman, who claimed to be held captive in a home.

"I've been abducted," she whispered to the dispatcher. "Please hurry."

The police who arrived at the scene not only rescued the woman who had placed the call, but also discovered two dead bodies – left there by Shawn Michael Grate, a 40-year-old man who had a reputation for being a "cold-blooded charmer." Grate also brought police to a third body, located in a wooded area by a ravine in neighbouring Richland County. And, as the investigation continued, police uncovered connections to two more murders.

"(He is) obviously a serial killer," said Marion County Sheriff Tim Bailey. "It's hard to believe others aren't out there."

The cold-blooded charmer

"He was charming. He was always smiling, and he had those big blue eyes," said Amy Smith, remembering Grate as a teenager in Marion, Ohio. "All the girls liked Shawn."

As irresistible as he was, multiple women recall experiencing Grate's dark side early on. By the age of 18, Grate had revealed himself to be jealous, controlling, and violent – and was even arrested for grabbing the throat of his young girlfriend.

When he was only 23, Grate broke into the home his pregnant 17-year-old girlfriend, where he choked her and, according to Marion police reports, threatened to kill her. And only eight months later, he hid all night under the girl's couch before assaulting her and her sister with a butcher knife.

"(Grate) told them to shut up because he was in control," reported an officer at the scene. "Then he said if anyone comes to the door, there will not be anyone here to answer it, so you better hope that no one knocks at the door."

In addition to this pregnancy, Grate is known to have fathered at least two other children. Two were with girlfriends in Marion, and the third is the product of a brief marriage in Mansfield. According to court documents, Grate's ex-wife said he once threatened that "if I can't see my daughter, then no one will."

Grate's criminal history is fairly extensive – but until 2016, he'd only spent about four years in prison for a burglary in Marion, violating early release conditions with an assault, and for domestic violence. Grate had also been charged several times with offences relating to drugs and alcohol.

Grate grew up in Marion County, the product of a broken home. His mother, Teresa McFarland, left his father, Terry Grate, in 1982 – and eventually relinquished custody of both Grate and his older brother, Ronald, to her ex-husband.

McFarland still resides in rural Ashland County, and has discussed her son in only one interview to date. She told the Daily Mail, a British tabloid, that her son changed after getting involved with drugs and spending time in prison – and added that for the past three years, Grate had been estranged from the rest of the family.

"Yes, he's good looking, but the devil's good looking, too," McFarland said. "He ain't got no red horns and all that stuff. You find out he's charming, and of course, that charm can charm the pants off anybody."

It's this charm that Grate uses to get what he wants. He's been described as lazy by many people who have recently come in contact with him – and rather than work, people say he prefers to take advantage of kind, vulnerable people, particularly women with money.

Wally Toward, a businessman in Mansfield who owns several properties, saw Grate attempt to move in with several of his female tenants.

"Grate always mistook kindness for weakness," Toward said. "He exploited kind people."

By his late 20s, Grate was beginning to show signs of mental health issues. According to Smith, Grate's teenage friend, he would frequently invest all his energy into a project before completely giving up on it after only a couple of weeks.

"He would just give up on everything," she said.

His erratic behaviour was a concern to a female friend of Smith's, who had dated Grate around 1999 but eventually broke up with him because he "wasn't acting right."

"He would get very, very depressed," Smith said. "My girlfriend would say, '(he) is not wanting to get off the couch. It's been days.'"

In 2005, Grate started dating another young woman named Christina Hildreth. The couple dated for about five years, and eventually lived together in Crawford County.

"He was very handsome and quite charming," she recalled. "He had a way of looking at you like you were the only person he saw."

However, after they moved into the same residence, Grate began to reveal his controlling, jealous tendencies – and it was hard for Hildreth to deal with.

"He started showing a side of himself that was cold and indifferent," she admitted. "He wanted me to himself."

It wasn't just his relationships with women that escalated, however. Tim Denis, who used to be a close friend of Grate's, said the friendship fell apart over a bad loan. When Denis refused to provide Grate with financial support, he received a string of angry text messages from his friend – and admitted the last message "still gives him chills.

"Meet the other me," Grate had messaged.

A growing threat

Following the divorce of his parents, Grate lived with his mother in Marion County, where he completed high school in 1995. At that time, he was a close friend of Smith's, who said she remembers him as her "go-to person" and a "shoulder to cry on."

"He was the one that came to a Halloween party dressed as a woman, making everyone laugh and has nothing but a smile on his face," she recalled. "That is the Shawn I know. That is the Shawn I want to remember."

Grate was the literal boy next door for Julia Pennington-Smith, who graduated from River Valley in 1995. She remembers Grate as one of her childhood best friends – not as a serial killer.

"I knew him from the time I was five years old," she said. "We grew up together. We were neighbours. We went to school together. We used to play backyard football, we used to play softball. They were like my brothers; I loved the family."

While Pennington-Smith said she hadn't been in contact with Grate since they graduated from high school, the two were friends on Facebook.

"I don't remember him being troubled," she said. "I don't remember him ever getting into any trouble. He lived a normal life."

But Grate's first adult arrest happened just weeks after he turned 18, while he was still in high school. While his juvenile record is unknown, there are police reports available detailing his early run-ins with the law.

The first arrest was the result of a domestic incident, after his girlfriend at the time claimed she had been trying to end the relationship for the past six months. However, the couple was still together and had a new baby when she reported a second domestic incident in January 1996.

"He seems to be involved in nonviolent crime except when dealing with females, especially those he is intimate with," said Tristin Kilgallon, who teaches a class on serial killers at Ohio Northern University, where he works as an assistant professor of criminal justice.

Later that same year, Grate was convicted of a felony charge after committing a burglary with a juvenile, and was sentenced to four years in prison. He served only seven months and was released early – but his violence continued to escalate.

In 1999, when he was 22, Grate's 17-year-old girlfriend told police that he had choked her nearly unconscious – while she was two months pregnant with his child.

"(His girlfriends) are getting younger... why? Are they easier to manipulate?" Kilgallon inquired. "He chokes her – this is up close and personal."

Still, the incident resulted in less than a month's worth of jailtime for Grate. Although the teenage girl's family pursued a restraining order against Grate, the young woman had the no-contact order removed just a few months later.

Even after Grate's second child was born, the relationship continued to struggle. His son was born in September, and only a month later, Grate threatened his son's mother and her sister with the butcher knife. During the struggle over the knife, both Grate and the young girl sustained minor to severe cuts.

"He steps it up," said Kilgallon. "He's using a weapon now."

This incident meant a longer period of incarceration for Grate, as his early release was revoked in 2000 and he was forced to serve what was left of his original four-year sentence. The prosecutor on the case said a separate prison term was initially sought for the new conviction, but the judge sentenced Grate to probation only.

In January 2003, Grate was released from prison again – and by October, he was already in more trouble with the law. Another domestic charge came as a result of a complaint received from the mother of Grate's second child, stating that he had choked her and forced her to perform a sex act on him. No sexual assault charges were laid, but Grate was charged with two counts of misdemeanor domestic violence – and went back to prison until May 2004.

Grate mostly laid low for the next couple years, with records showing nothing but minor run-ins with the law – but Grate has admitted now that his first kill was in 2005, an unidentified woman who was distributing newspapers and magazines in his neighbourhood.

In 2005, Grate started dating Hildreth, who he moved in with a year later. He was upset that her children were living with them as well, Hildreth said, but said he was primarily just mentally abusive – although she does recall some physical violence, as well.

The worst incident happened in June 2010, Hildreth said, when Grate assaulted her repeatedly – with multiple blows to her face, and grabbing her roughly by the throat. She even fractured her hand in an attempt to defend herself from the falling blows.

Grate did eventually bring Hildreth to the emergency room, and they told the hospital staff that she'd fallen. However, as soon as she was left alone with a nurse, Hildreth explained what had actually happened. While police were informed immediately, Grate managed to escape arrest temporarily – but was arrested four days later, when Hildreth told the authorities that she was concerned Grate was hiding inside her couch.

Grate was charged with a first-degree misdemeanor domestic violence, and received a sentence of 180 days in jail. Despite the issuing of a protection order, Grate continued to call Hildreth from jail, and sent letters that he addressed to her cats. Hildreth, however, ended their relationship after incident, and to this day, believes it kept both her and her children alive.

"Before that night, I feared he would kill me," she recalled. "That night only strengthened that fear. I now believe more than ever had I not left him, I would be dead or one of my children would be."

The family man

Grate settled down with a new partner in 2011, a 28-year-old Mansfield woman named Amber Nicole Bowman. The couple were married and living together in the ranch house she owned when she gave birth to their daughter in July 2012.

Despite her young marriage and a brand new baby, though, Bowman filed for divorce in October 2012, citing "serious and unfortunate differences" in the separation agreement filed in December of that year.

Bowman sought a restraining order just a few months later, in April 2013 – claiming Grate had been calling her at work and making threats that if he couldn't see his daughter, "no one else will." He demanded money from Bowman, to "help him get back on his feet." He was also not paying child support for any of the three children he had fathered so far.

That June, the Richland County Child Support Enforcement Agency informed the county's domestic relations court that they had reason to believe that Grate was unemployed, and by September, a contempt of court order was issued against him for failure to seek work. He'd apparently been moving from place to place in Mansfield, but was technically homeless.

"He was not mentally disabled, he was not physically disabled," Toward said, who frequently worried Grate would steal rent money from his female tenants. "He could hold a job if he chose to, but instead of that he always chose to maneuver people to con them into helping him."

During this time frame, Grate was getting to know two women – Rebekah Leicy and Candice Cunningham. Leicy was a prostitute who worked in the Third Street area, the same area where Grate's ex-girlfriend Amber White used to work.

"He picked me up, I used to prostitute," White recalled, adding that he would only have about $10 or $20 to spend on sexual favours. "He was shy. He didn't talk (during sex), and he wanted the lights off. I was mean to him because I was strung out on drugs and he just disappeared."

Originally, Leicy's death was ruled as a drug overdose when her body was discovered in March 2015, in a wooded area of Ashland

County. After speaking with Grate following his arrest in September 2016, however, police have reopened the case and are investigating the possibility that Grate may be responsible for her death.

Cunningham and Grate were living together in Mansfield when she went missing in June 2015. When he was arrested, Grate informed police that they could find the body of a woman near a burned out house in nearby Madison Township. The body has yet to be identified, but evidence indicates it is likely Cunningham.

Foiled

Grate claims he wanted to marry the woman who called 911 on September 13 – a call that led to her rescue, and his arrest. The abduction victim, who has yet to be identified, occasionally played badminton with Grate at her apartment complex in Ashland – until she was kidnapped and forced to endured two days of involuntary sexual activity before she was able to place a call to police.

The chilling 19-minute call reveals a terrified woman whispering to a dispatcher in a quavering voice – identifying Grate by name, describing a nearby laundromat, informing police that Grate was armed with a taser, and reassuring the dispatcher that she was not bleeding, "anymore."

"I'm in the bedroom with him," she said, her voice hushed. "I'm scared."

The abducted woman lived in the same area as one of the other women whose body police discovered at the home, 29-year-old Elizabeth Griffith. According to Griffith's friends, she and Grate had dated, and Griffith had been missing since August 16.

"The short time I talked to her she cried several times, just about life and how she couldn't find anyone to love her," Grate said in a rare interview from jail in October 2016. "She had a mental illness."

Police discovered her body stuffed in an upstairs closet in the vacant home, and another body in the basement – Stacey Stanley, a

43-year-old woman from Greenwich who had been reported missing only days earlier.

According to Stanley's son, Kurtis, she hadn't come home after going out for a coffee and stopping at a gas station with a flat tire. Grate said he "helped" the woman before taking her back to the home where he had been squatting.

"It is a sad situation, especially the way she died," said Stanley's uncle, Argil Stanley. "She was beaten to death. The cops said she was unrecognizable from the beating."

After police uncovered the two bodies inside the house, Grate admitted to killing another woman in Richland County, and proceeded to bring police to her body – the body believed to be Candice Cunningham. He confessed that he'd also killed Leicy and another woman whose name he couldn't remember, back in 2005. His first kill, he said.

While the abduction victim who called 911 has not been identified publicly, her family has spoken out about the incident – and claim they will never forgive Grate for what he put her through. The victim's father said the family was fully supportive of the death penalty, which Grate has admitted that he deserves.

According to the victim's brother, Grate preyed on the woman's faith to develop a relationship with her – and eventually kidnap her.

"If somebody wanted to be a predator, like this guy obviously was, he could just feed off that and sense that," said the victim's brother. "As long as she would have somebody who would listen to that, oh, he could do whatever he wanted, manipulate however he wanted. That's the way I pretty much believe it went down."

Grate did admit to police that he is religious, as were a number of his victims. He said the women were lonely, and seemed to have lost their way – even claiming that they didn't even want to go on living.

In a confession, Grate explained that he would hug his victims and remind them that "we are all in this together," before choking them.

According to Grate, he would give his victims one last opportunity to beg for their lives – and if they didn't, he would end it for them.

So far, Grate has admitted to killing five women, and claims four of them were "choked out." His first victim, however, was stabbed in the throat. Grate believes her name was Dana, but her body has not been identified yet.

According to Grate, "Dana" delivered magazines and newspapers throughout his mother's neighbourhood in Marion, Ohio – but was "scheming" his mother out of her subscription.

"I remember her trying to sell them to me," Grate recalled. "Me and my mom would be on the porch and she'd try to sell them. My mom said she wasn't getting her subscriptions delivered."

Since he had company coming over soon, he didn't have time to strangle his first victim. Instead, he stabbed her in the throat and left her in the basement. Eventually, he brought her body out to Victory Road in Marion, where it stayed until it was discovered two years later. Currently, the only information the Marion County sheriff's department has to help make an identification is a sketch.

Grate also confessed to killing Leicy ten years later, although her death had already been ruled as drug related. According to Grate, the two had met at a bar, and she'd tried to steal $4 from him while he was in the restroom – so he strangled her, like the other three more recent victims.

Cunningham was killed in a vacant house the couple was squatting in, according to Grate, and he went back and burned the house down to hide her body. Police records show that the house had been destroyed in a suspicious fire on June 21 – the day after Grate successfully fled an officer who'd stopped him on a felony child support warrant.

"We were seeing each other for about seven months," Grate said of Cunningham. "She was pretty violent and suicidal, I turned her into a psych ward for about a week. Then we fought at the house in Richland for three to four days. Then the next day we'd get up and go for walks.

She could have run off and told police at any time ... She would take handfuls of pills at a time and I would give her the water."

Police are still collecting evidence and DNA to connect Grate to all five murders. Currently, he's been indicted on 23 charges – including aggravated murder for the deaths of Stanley and Griffith and kidnapping for the abduction of the victim who escaped. Each murder count carries the possibility of a prison term of 15 years to life, and the kidnapping charge could be punishable by 3 to 11 years in prison.

Charges have not been filed on the other three murders Grate claims to be responsible for. According to Ashland County Prosecutor Chris Tunnell, a "large volume" of evidence has been collected by the state Bureau of Criminal Identification and Investigation, the Ashland Police Department, and other agencies.

"A clear vision of WHY."

About a month after his arrest, Grate sent two letters to a Cleveland reporter, acknowledging his part in the five killings – and providing what he claimed was his motive for murdering the women. The letters were a response to a request for an on-camera interview.

"That sounds scary in facing myself even more," Grate's first letter stated. "The mirror has been enough but having more questions hitting me straight on could and would only help to understand me better."

The second letter explains Grate's motive for committing a "horrible act of violent behavior," stating that while in jail, he was able to gain a "clear vision of WHY."

"They were already dead, just their bodies were flopping wherever it can flop but their minds were already dead!" Grate wrote. "The state took their minds. Once they started receiving their monthly cheques."

Grate blames "government assistance" for robbing his victims of their "minds," and said that while he applied for government assistance five years ago, all he received was a $197 food card over a year and a half.

"Many bodies received 700," he wrote – using the words "people," "victims," and "bodies" interchangeably throughout the letters.

The letters are also full of Bible verses, specifically passages from the Book of Revelation and Hebrews.

"I feel I deserve the death penalty," he said in an October 2016 interview from prison, "but I also feel I can help some people in here ... I'm just trying to free myself of what I've done. I'm afraid of the death penalty ... I'd like to die on my own and not by the state."

Grate's mother, McFarland, said that she feels terrible for the trauma her son inflicted on his victims – and their families.

"it feels like a nightmare," she said. "I pray for the families. It's like a death to me too, and I have to grieve."

Jekyll and Hyde

Grate has claimed he feels some remorse for the murders – "50/50," he told a reporter.

According to Kilgallon, Grate is a perfect example of a killer motivated by a need for power and control. Often, he said, these killers are intelligent and charismatic – and master manipulators. When manipulation tactics fail, however, they will turn to violence.

Kilgallon added Grate was successful in covering his tracks each time, and despite frequently physically and sexually abusing his partners, they stayed with him – sometimes even for years. While Grate may have a specific victim type, he may prey on specific women simply because he finds them "easy targets."

"What we know about men, specifically that are violent against women, is that they feel entitled to be violent or justified in their violence," said Nancy Radcliffe, HelpLine of Delaware and Morrow Counties' director of sexual assault services.

Radcliffe's experience in the area of intimate partner violence spans more than 25 years, and while she has not assessed Grate's case personally, said he may fit the "Jekyll and Hyde" model of domestic abusers.

"On the outside, on any given day, they seem to be very outstanding members of society – people that you would look up to or wouldn't be at all threatened by," she explained. "But there's this other persona that comes out from time to time, and usually towards the person that they want to see it."

Toward, who claimed he's always prided himself on his ability to read people, admitted that he "missed the boat" when it came to Grate. And while he has had confrontations with a number of people during his time delivering subpoenas for local attorneys, he doesn't like to think about the fact that he made have had some "vivid discussions" with a potential serial killer.

"When I look back and try to analyze why I could not read him was because he is truly evil," Toward said. "For every Mother Theresa, there's a Charlie Manson – and he is Mansfield's Charlie Manson. He is a sociopath. You can't read a sociopath because there's no soul to read."

GAINESVILLE RIPPER: The True Story of Danny Rolling

NIKKI MARSHALL

They called him the Gainesville Ripper.

In 1990, Danny Rolling murdered four University of Florida students and a Santa Fe Community College student in their apartments with a United States Marine Corps military-style KBAR knife by stabbing, slicing, mutilating, raping, and even decapitating some of his victims. He had also been linked to and found guilty of killing a family of three in his home town in 1989: a crime for which another person was initially arrested. Rolling was later apprehended in conjunction with a botched grocery store robbery and later pled guilty to all of the grisly murders during jury selection in 1994. After an unsuccessful appeal of his death sentence he was ultimately executed via lethal injection on 25 October 2006.

Early Life

Daniel Harold Rolling was born on 26 May 1954 in Shreveport, Louisiana, to Claudia and James Rolling. Claudia had married James in 1953 when she was 19 and became pregnant with Danny only two weeks later, much to her husband's chagrin. During her pregnancy James had physically assaulted her several times. Whereas she moved to her parents' house due to the violence on several occasions, he followed her and begged her to return home which she did—each time.

After Danny was born his father's attitude remain unchanged as James frequently yelled at his infant son. Once, when Danny pulled himself across the floor on his bottom instead of crawling, his father grabbed his foot and shoved the toddler across the hallway.

Danny had a brother, Kevin, who was a year younger. When Danny was four his mother left James again and moved to Columbus, Georgia, after an argument resulting from James' repeatedly turning off the television while Claudia was watching escalated to the point that he punched his wife, cutting her lip. After a six-month separation Claudia went back. She left and returned again after four years. Then the Rollings moved to Shreveport, Louisiana.

Claudia tried to shield her sons from their father's abuse by ensuring that they had already eaten before he had come home because he would constantly abuse them for "imagined transgressions" such as not sitting right, not holding their silverware properly, or even breathing wrong. When James was physically violent to his sons—either with a belt or his fists—they could not cry for fear of even harsher punishment. Danny received the brunt of the abuse; being yelled at daily and whipped a few times per week.

Claudia left again one Christmas when Danny was in the third grade but, again, didn't stay away long. She had a nervous breakdown soon after and was hospitalized for a while. During that time Danny was ill and missed a lot of school. His teacher told his father that he needed to repeat that year and should get some counseling for his issues. Instead of helping his son, James berated him for being a failure.

Crimes

Rolling had a rather long history of prior violent felonies before he began to kill: a 1976 conviction in Mississippi for armed robbery; a 1979 conviction in Georgia for two counts of armed robbery; a 1980 Alabama conviction for robbery; a 1991 Hillsborough County, Florida, conviction for three counts of attempted robbery with a firearm and two counts of aggravated assault on a police officer; and a 1992 federal conviction for armed bank robbery. He served eight years in prison and later stated that he wanted to kill eight people; one for each year of his prior incarceration.

The Grissoms

In November 1989, while Rolling still resided in his hometown, an attacker stabbed to death three members of the Grissom family in November 1989. Tom, 55, his daughter Julie, 24, and his nephew Sean, 8; just one year before Rolling came to Florida. The killer entered the house through an unlocked door.

Gainesville, Florida, has been described as a smallish city replete with pretty homes and, was actually ranked as the 13th best place to live in the United States in the late 1980s according to *Money* magazine. Once Rolling arrived, however, Gainesville became a town crippled with dread as the University of Florida was shut down for an entire week and students lived in fear, stayed in large groups, purchased mace and guns, and put triple locks on their doors while helicopters with spotlights circled above at night. Sorority houses hired full-time security guards and residents made sure to lock their doors. This peaceful haven had been named "Grisly Gainesville" after the murders.

Rolling had stated that he wanted to become a "superstar." His "murder kit" included his KBAR knife, duct tape, a handgun, and a screwdriver to gain entry into the victims' homes.

Christina Powell and Sonja Larson

The screwdriver and gun were not needed when he noticed that the door was unlocked at unit #113 in the Williamsburg Village Apartments. When he entered in the early morning hours of 24 August 1990 he found 17-year-old Christina Powell asleep on the downstairs couch. He crept upstairs where he discovered 18-year-old Sonja Larson asleep as well in her bedroom. He paused momentarily to decide which of the young women he wanted to rape before attacking Larson, stabbing her in the upper chest area and placing some duct tape over her mouth. Rolling continued to stab Larson as she unsuccessfully struggled against him as evidenced by numerous defensive wounds to her arms and a deep slash to her left thigh. She died shortly thereafter.

Rolling then turned his attention to Powell. He placed a double strip of duct tape over her mouth and restrained her wrists behind her back, also with duct tape. He cut off her clothing and underwear with the KBAR and raped her at knifepoint. When he was finished he forced Powell to lie face down on the floor and then stabbed her five times in the back, killing her.

Rolling then posed his victims' bodies: Larson was on her bed with her arms above her head. Both victims had been mutilated.

Officer Ray Barber arrived at the residence at approximately 4:00 p.m. on 26 August after Frank and Patricia Powell from Jacksonville called them as they couldn't get a hold of their daughter. Further, nobody had seen her and her car was still parked by the apartments. Similarly, Larson's mother reported that her daughter failed to call her as was previously arranged.

Soon thereafter 20 officers were on the scene including Police Chief Wayland Clifton. They estimated the young women's deaths as occurring between 11:30 p.m. 23 August and 4:00 p.m. 25 August. During the initial investigation Elsa Streppe, who also shared the apartment with Powell and Larson, returned home. She was escorted from the scene where she was informed as to what happened to her roommates and almost collapsed from the realization of how close she came to being murdered as well.

Before the police left they were summoned to another crime scene where deputies Keith O'Hara and Gail Barber from the Alachua County Sheriff's Office were waiting.

Christa Hoyt

The next morning, 25 August, Rolling broke into 18-year-old Christa Hoyt's apartment which was located approximately two miles from the first crime scene by prying open the sliding glass door with his screwdriver. Rolling waited in Hoyt's living room. He had already peeked into her bedroom a few days earlier. Upon Hoyt's arrival home at 11:00 a.m. Rolling surprised her from behind and placed her in a chokehold from which he was able to subdue the young college student. He taped her mouth and hands and forced her into the bedroom where he cut off her clothes and undergarments, forced her onto the bed, and raped her at knifepoint.

He then turned Hoyt over and stabbed her through the back, rupturing her aorta. Not unlike his other victims, Rolling posed Hoyt's body. Her decapitated head was found atop a bookshelf in her bedroom. She was propped sitting up on her bed and bent over at the waist. Her nipples had been sliced off and Rolling left them on the bed next to her. Her torso had also been sliced open from her chest to her pubic bone.

Police were dispatched to Hoyt's apartment when she failed to show up for her midnight shift as a records clerk at the Alachua County Sheriff's Office. It was 12:30 a.m. and she wasn't answering her phone. Deputy Barber knew her coworker Hoyt. While the deputies were there manager Elbert Hoover came out to investigate as he heard them knocking on her door and calling out her name. Hoover saw that the gate was damaged and the chain-link fence was down and knew something was wrong. They tried the sliding glass door and it was locked from the inside.

The deputies noticed that the bamboo shades covering Hoyt's glass door did not reach the floor and when they looked underneath it they saw what appeared to be a naked body seated on the edge of the bed, bent over at the waist with a pool of blood at the shoes-and-socks-clad feet. The body didn't have a head.

At 1:00 p.m. Sergeant Allen Baxter and Lieutenant Nobles arrived on scene. O'Hara and Barber briefed them and stated that they had heard water running from inside and perhaps the killer might still be there. After 30 minutes additional backup arrived and authorities were ready to enter the building.

When they first entered through the front door they did so cautiously in case the perpetrator was still inside. They heard the drip of the shower in the bathroom but nobody was there; however, there were bloodstains on the shower floor. As they left the bathroom they saw Hoyt's decapitated head facing them on the bedroom bookshelf. In her bedroom police saw Hoyt's headless corpse sitting at the end of the bed with her nipples on the bed beside her. The killer was not on the premises. When they attended to Hoyt and sat her up she had been carefully sliced from the breastbone to the pubic bone.

Chief Clifton arrived on scene and wanted to know whether Hoyt's murder was connected to the murders of Powell and Larson. Preliminary investigation confirmed his suspicion. At both scenes the girls' underwear was missing. Despite Rolling's attempt to remove the duct tape from the victims, evidence of adhesive was present on all three bodies. A four-to-six inch knife blade was used on all three girls. Also, body parts were missing at both scenes.

The following Monday, Sheriff Lu Hindery of the Alachua County Sheriff's Office and Chief Clifton from the Gainesville Police Department created a combined task force to include the best investigators and crime scene investigators and technicians from both departments along with representatives from the Florida Department of Law Enforcement and the Florida Highway Patrol, as well as ten of the top Federal Bureau of Investigation's criminal behavioral specialists. The task force was headed by Lieutenant R.B. Ward from the Gainesville Police Department, Captain Andy Hamilton from the Alachua County Sheriff's Office, and Special Agent J.O. Jackson from the Florida Department of Law Enforcement.

The first news conference was held Monday night where police attempted to quell the panic that had gripped Gainesville; however, in an effort to ensure that valuable details about the crimes were kept under wraps there was little they could say to alleviate the fright.

When two more bodies were found the next day, 28 August, the panic and fear had reached its apex and when word spread that one of the victims was male, nobody felt safe.

Tracy Paules and Manuel Taboada

At approximately 3:00 a.m. on 27 August Rolling broke into high school friends Tracy Paules' and Manuel Taboada's—both 23 years of age—apartment at the Gatorwood Apartments by, again, prying open the glass sliding door with his screwdriver. In the first bedroom Rolling found Taboada asleep and proceeded to stab the young college student through the solar plexus which subsequently penetrated his thoracic vertebra. Taboada snapped awake and tried to fight back against his attacker. Rolling repeatedly stabbed his arms, hands, chest, legs, and face and the young man died from the attack.

Having heard the commotion, Paules approached her roommate's bedroom and, after seeing Rolling, ran back to her own bedroom and tried to lock the door. Blood-covered Rolling followed her, broke through her bedroom door, subdued her, taped her mouth and hands, cut off her clothes, and raped her at knifepoint. When he was finished he turned her over and killed her with three stabs to her back. He then cleaned himself off and posed her body like the others.

One of Taboada's friends, Tommy Carrol, went to check on his friends at approximately 7:00 a.m. on Tuesday 28 August after being told by another friend, Khris Pascarella, that they haven't been reached for a couple of days. When Carrol arrived maintenance man Christopher Smith met him and subsequently opened the door with a master key. They immediately saw Paules' naked and bloody body lying in the hallway between the bedrooms and there was a dark bag on the floor next to her. He slammed the door shut, locked it, and left to call the police. When police arrived the door was unlocked and the bag was gone, thus leading to speculation that perhaps Rolling had been interrupted before he could mutilate Paules' body.

Save for Taboada, all of the Gainesville victims were petite brunettes with brown eyes.

Edward Humphrey

Initially, the police reported that they had their prime suspect in custody; a man named Edward Humphrey, then 18-years-old, who had been in the wrong place at the wrong time. Humphrey was an emotionally disturbed man with a history of odd behavior and violent outbursts. He served to be a red herring in the case.

Humphrey had once lived in the same apartment complex as Paules and Taboada and had been asked to leave after he fought with his roommates who stated that Humphreys was "weird and walked in his sleep." When asked to leave, Humphreys became violent and threw a chair at them. At his next apartment down the street he had gotten into trouble by going into other tenants' apartments uninvited and when they locked him out he resorted to peeping through their curtains.

In early August, prior to the murders, Humphrey was arrested in Ordway, Colorado, for disorderly conduct. He was held in custody before his grandmother Elna Hlavaty came to bring him back to Gainesville. While trying to find him an apartment, Humphrey subjected his grandmother to his violent behavior. Additionally, students in the area had notified police of Humphrey's harassment and arguments, including one incident where he wielded a penknife at a fraternity house when they wouldn't let him in.

Humphrey had become the police's prime suspect and he was subject to round-the-clock surveillance. Toward the end of summer Humphrey had a violent argument with his grandmother wherein he hit her. His mother called the police and convinced her own mother to sign a complaint against her grandson for aggravated assault. Humphrey was arrested and interrogated by FBI agents for 24 hours without an attorney. In fact, when the public defender assigned to Humphrey arrived, agents sent him away stating that no arrest had been made in regard to the Gainesville murders as there was no evidence and that he was being arrested on the assault charge only.

Humphrey was sent to the Brevard County Jail in Sharpes, Florida, and held in lieu of a $1 million bond; very high for a first-time offender on a minor assault charge. As he awaited his trial the media blitz against him commenced with the publication of his mugshot coupled with various reports dubbing him the Gainesville killer.

As the investigation continued, police found no evidence on Humphrey's person, in his apartment or car, or even at his grandmother's house. Despite the complete absence of any evidence that Humphrey was responsible for the murders the police maintained that he was their prime suspect. When there were no additional murders after his arrest, police became more convinced, as were the media.

Luckily for Humphrey, Rolling was found before the case against him was complete. Humphrey, however, was convicted of assault on 10 October and sentenced to 22 months at a mental hospital in Chattahoochee, Florida. He was released on 18 September 1991 and was still considered a suspect until Rolling was sentenced in 1994. Until then his name was never officially cleared nor did he or his family receive any public apology for the anguish caused to him and his family.

Arrest and Conviction

Shortly after the murders, Rolling narrowly avoided arrest after robbing the First National Bank. Despite being identified Rolling was not considered to be a suspect in the murders. Rolling was first noticed by police as he and new friend Tony Danzy—who supplied Rolling with drugs—were headed to their campsite near the woods on Archer Road, near Hoyt's apartment. While Danzy waited for the police, Rolling ran. At Rolling's campsite and in his tent they found several items of evidence that would later link Rolling to the five murders; however, at that time the only item that caught their interest was a bag of money covered in pink dye.

Rolling resorted to what he knew best to get out of town. He burgled student Christopher Osborne's apartment, stole his 1978 Buick Regal, and headed toward Tampa. In Tampa, Rolling burgled a number of houses; not getting anything truly useful but leaving a large trail of evidence including fingerprints and hair. He robbed a convenience store and was almost apprehended but, once again, ran into the woods. He stole another car and headed to Ocala where on 8 September 1990 he attempted to rob a Winn Dixie supermarket during the peak of Saturday afternoon business. While Rolling forced store manager Randy Wilson to empty the office safe at gunpoint, the store's bookkeeper was on her way back to work. When told at the entrance that a robbery was in progress she called the police and they were en route before he even left the store. Wilson had managed to tell police in which direction Rolling had fled and in what vehicle.

A high-speed chase by police ensued and led to Rolling crashing his car and trying to escape on foot through a nearby office but as he exited through a back door the police were waiting. He tried unsuccessfully to run again and was subsequently arrested.

From the moment he was arrested Rolling was completely cooperative with police and prison authorities; however, on 1 January 1991 he ripped a toilet from its base in a fit of anger and threw it across the prison dayroom which made authorities believe that there was more to Rolling than they initially thought.

Three days later, on 11 September, the Gainesville Ripper story no longer appeared on the first page of the newspaper and the community was no longer under threat.

While incarcerated Rolling would draw disturbing pictures and even penned a graphic book entitled, "The Making of a Serial Killer," with a woman who was his fiancée for a while. He also was extremely loose-lipped among the inmate population and a number of inmates sought out the investigating team to relate Rolling's stories and alleged confessions which ranged from regretful admissions to bragging, depending upon his mood at the time.

One inmate, Bobby Lewis, became Rolling's friend. Lewis was the only man to have ever escaped from Florida's death row and Rolling knew that if he ever wanted to get out of prison he would have to escape. Rolling allegedly confessed to Lewis all of the explicit details of the murders and told him that he had decided to kill while previously incarcerated during the 1980. Rolling blamed his father's abuse and neglect, sexual abuse he experienced in prison, and his ex-wife for his bad side. He and Lewis planned for Rolling to fake his own suicide so they could be housed in the same ward to solidify their escape plans.

On 31 January 1993, Rolling told the investigators that he wanted to confess: through Lewis. In a three-hour confession Lewis related what Rolling had told him and Rolling simply confirmed what Lewis was saying. Rolling blamed his heinous acts on an evil alter persona that he called "Gemini" which, of course, the investigators dismissed because of the fact that Rolling had watched the *Exorcist, Part III* during the week of the Gainesville murders and in it the killer was known as Gemini and had decapitated and disemboweled a female victim.

After the confession Lewis was moved from the ward which caused Rolling to feel betrayed. Rolling found a new confidante in Rusty Binstead but instead of only talking about his heinous acts he wrote them all down in a letter; the original he gave to Binstead with instructions to make a copy and to give the original back to him. Binstead, instead, told one of his neighbors to call out "Shakedown" during which time Binstead flushed his toilet to make Rolling believe that he had flushed the letter.

Rolling's trial was set to commence in 1994 and his attorney Public Defender C. Richard Parker sought to get a change of venue for the trial which was denied. Since his story had been so sensationalized by the media across the country there was no way he would have received a fair trial with jurors who harbored no knowledge and/or bias about his crimes. Additionally, many pieces of evidence including statements Rolling made to the police without counsel present and items collected from his home without a warrant were ruled admissible in court. In total, police had accumulated over 1,500 pieces of evidence.

Rolling wanted to plead guilty; however, Parker tried to convince him that there were several mitigating factors that may save Rolling from a death sentence if he would stick with his not-guilty plea and that if he did, in fact, plead guilty then not only would there be a stronger chance that Rolling would receive a death sentence but it would be virtually impossible to have his conviction overturned in an appeal. He would only be able to appeal his sentence.

Rolling decided to plead guilty the week before his trial was scheduled to begin. He signed a three-page plea form at the Florida State Prison to make it official. Some say that this act demonstrated some remorse for his actions because Rolling said that he didn't want the crime scene photographs to be shown in court.

In court on 15 February, Rolling's decision to plead guilty was met with shocked silence. The only business left was to select the jury that would decide whether he would live or die.

The jury was charged with weighing aggravating factors presented by the prosecution against mitigating factors presented by the defense. Under Florida law there were 11 possible aggravating circumstances and only one needed to be proven for the jury to determine that a death sentence was warranted. As for mitigating factors, the defense had no restrictions of what type of evidence could be presented as such. All that had to occur was for jurors to determine whether the mitigating factors outweighed the prosecution's case and only seven of the 12 jurors had to agree as to whether Rolling should be sentenced to death. The judge then bore the onus of deciding whether or not he would accept said recommendation.

Opening arguments for the sentencing phase commenced on Tuesday 7 March 1994 with the prosecution asserting that it would be successful in presenting five of the possible 11 aggravating factors: the crimes were premeditated and cold-blooded; they were committed during sexual battery; they were "particularly heinous, atrocious and cruel"; the offender had a prior history of felony convictions; and the crimes "were committed for the purpose of escaping detection or avoiding arrests"—especially in the Larson and Taboada cases.

On the other side, the defense sought to prove the mitigating circumstances that Rolling suffered mental illness at the time he committed the murders; that the crimes were committed under extreme stress; that Rolling was raised in an abusive household; that he had a history of drug and alcohol abuse; and that he showed remorse.

Despite Rolling's hope that the crime scene photos would not be presented in court as evidence the prosecution had no intention of sparing the jury and observers every grisly detail of Rolling's crimes. State attorney Rod Smith presented considerable evidence including DNA matches based upon semen at the crime scenes; items found at Rolling's campsite which included the screwdriver that forensic examiners stated matched the tool marks at the crime scenes, duct tape, and black pants stained with Taboada's blood; a handwriting match between Rolling's confession and a note found at one of the scenes; all of the details of the murders Rolling had told other inmates; proof that Rolling purchased a KBAR knife that matched the one that was used in the murders; Rolling's handwritten confession given to Binstead; and the videotaped confession Rolling made through Lewis. Rolling's prior felonies were also detailed: eight counts of armed robbery; one count of attempted robbery; one count of armed bank robbery; and two counts of aggravated assault of a police officer which occurred in four states. Further, Smith described in detail how Rolling tortured his victims, how he informed his victims what he was going to do to them before he killed them, and how the murders occurred during rape. Smith also told jurors that the evidence proved "beyond every reasonable doubt" that Rolling was guilty of all of the murders and deserved the death penalty.

John J. Kearns—one of Florida's best public defenders in 1986—was tasked with convincing the jury that enough mitigating factors existed to not sentence Rolling to die. These included that Rolling was a victim of constant physical and emotional abuse during his childhood, was mentally ill, and, therefore, not accountable for his actions. To prove these assertions Kearns presented a number of friends and relatives as well as a plethora of psychiatrists who had spent over 50 hours evaluating Rolling. Rolling's mother, Claudia, through a videotaped deposition, discussed the environment during her son's childhood. The pressing question was whether Rolling was traumatized enough as a child to absolve him of full responsibility for his actions. Whereas the psychiatrists testified that he did, in fact, have a severe personality disorder and functioned at the maturity level of a 15-year-old, they also testified that he did not suffer from an evil alter ego or multiple personalities and was fully aware of the criminality of his actions during and after the murders.

On 30 March, Rolling confessed to the triple murder of the Grissoms in Shreveport and on the same day James Rolling was cited for battery of his wife during a domestic dispute.

Rolling was sentenced to death based upon the judge's assertion that his emotional disorder was "a non-statutory mitigating factor" that didn't merit much consideration and the aggravating factors far outweighed the mitigating ones.

Appeals

Rolling appealed the constitutionality of his sentence on a number of levels. He raised six specific claims: that the trial court abused its discretion in denying his request for a change of venue and violated his Sixth Amendment right to be fairly tried by an impartial jury; that the trial court erred in denying Rolling's motion to suppress his statements which were obtained in violation of his Sixth Amendment right to counsel; that the trial court erred in denying his motion to sever and conduct three separate sentencing proceedings; that the trial court erred in denying his motion to suppress the evidence found inside of his tent at the campsite because the warrantless search violated his Fourth Amendment rights; that the trial court erred in finding that Larson's murder was especially heinous, atrocious, or cruel which represented one of the aggravating factors; and that the trial court gave an invalid and unconstitutional jury instruction on said heinous, atrocious, or cruel aggravating circumstance. The Florida Supreme

Court denied all motions and the United States Supreme Court denied Rolling's final appeal prior to his execution.

Rolling's appellate attorney, Baya Harrison, helped with his client's wish to clear the name of another man who had been suspected in the Shreveport deaths of the Grissoms; Edward Humphrey, who the police initially believed to be guilty of the attacks. Just prior to his execution, Rolling gave police a written confession that he, in fact, was the Grissoms' killer and wrote that he, alone was guilty and he wished that he could bring them back. Louisiana chose not to serve the arrest warrant on Rolling because the Florida case was much stronger. Members of the Grissom family attended Rolling's execution.

Execution

Just prior to his execution Rolling sought guidance and spiritual advice from a minister of the Pentacostal church as he was raised Pentacostal; however, he stated that he swung between a deep faith and pure evil.

Rolling's last meal consisted of lobster tail, butterflied shrimp, baked potato, strawberry cheesecake, and sweet tea.

On 25 October 2006 at approximately 6:00 p.m., Rolling entered the death room.

While restrained atop a gurney awaiting his execution by lethal injection, Rolling turned his head and looked at Ricky Paules, the mother of one of his victims, Tracy Paules, before starting to sing, "None greater than thee, Oh Lord. None greater than thee," as the drugs that would end his life were pumped into his arm. He sang—and spoke of seeing "through a glass now, darkly" in reference to St. Paul—even after the microphone was turned off. He never expressed any remorse, sorrow, or regret for the murders in Gainesville he committed 16 years ago; nor did he ask his victims' families—many of them were in attendance—for forgiveness. There were at least a dozen family members in the witness room along with approximately 30 other observers who indicated that the only comparison that could be drawn from the deaths of Rolling's victims to his own was that he, too, was bound and unable to move. However, he was neither ambush attacked as he slept nor were his bones chipped and cut because he was stabbed so hard with a military KBAR knife. Other than that he got off pretty easily.

Rolling was pronounced dead at 6:13 p.m.; 13 minutes after he started singing and two minutes after his body ceased quivering and his face became slack, puffy, and discolored. He was 52 years old.

Aftermath

Rolling and the Gainesville murders are the subjects of profiler John Philpin's and journalist John Donnelly's book *Beyond Murder* (1995). He was also the subject of an episode of *Body of Evidence: From the Case Files of Dayle Hinman* and is widely thought to have been the inspiration for the original 1996 screenplay for the movie *Scream*.

Rolling's motives were never truly identified.

BURY THEM ALIVE : THE TRUE STORY OF SERIAL KILLER TIFFANY COLE

JESSICA WINSTON

When James "Reggie" and Carol Sumner moved to Jacksonville, Florida for their retirement, they had visions of good health and happiness. They never thought that their overnight invitation to long-time South Carolina neighbor, Tiffany Cole, would end up the way it did; With the Sumner couple being buried alive.

Reggie and Carol Sumner were high school sweethearts in North Charleston, South Carolina. They were the kind of couple that everyone envied as they walked down the hall. Unfortunately, their lives pulled them in different directions. Reggie decided to serve his country in the navy. After finishing his tour, he got married and landed a job with the railroad. Carol also married and became a devoted mother, however, her first marriage ended in divorce, and her second nearly killed her. In 1987, after years of abuse, her husband at the time shot her seven times in their home before driving away and turning the gun on himself. Her daughter, Rhonda Alford, just ten years old at that time, spent almost a year helping her mother recover from her wounds. She had to help her bathe, dress, and take care of the house. After taking eight years to fully recover, Carol went back to work as soon as she was able. For over twenty-five years she was a civil servant at the Citadel and the Charleston Air Force Base. She also worked a second job at night at a Belk department store, among other jobs she would take when needed. She did whatever she had to in order to make ends meet. Shortly after her recovery, she found out that the blood transfusion she had received during her previous trauma had given her Hepatitis C. She was angry because she felt as though she could not escape her late ex-husband, but she refused to let it ruin her life. She soon started a new job at a cable company and it was during this time that her life finally changed for the better. Nearly forty years after they'd left high school, a chance encounter brought Carol and Reggie together again. One night in 2000, a phone call was made to the cable company where Carol was working, which she received. After talking with the customer Carol and learning his name, she realized that he also sounded just like the Reggie she remembered. So she asked him if he was the same Reggie Sumner who attended Garrett High school in South Charleston. It was. They decided that they should get together after not seeing each other in so long. This time, though they were inseparable. Like "teenagers in love", a quick courtship led to love and then marriage in 2001 with a ceremony at Carol's home in West Ashley. Carol's daughter has said of Reggie "he was just a very gentle, kind and giving spirit. You could not ask for a better friend, husband or stepfather." Eventually, after retiring, the couple decided to move from South Carolina to Jacksonville, Florida. Reggie had previously bought a house during his days working for CSX railroad and as he was a "brittle" diabetic in frail health, he thought he would be more comfortable in the warmer climate. Carol agreed. "She only went down there to honor her husband," Rhonda said. Before moving, they decided to sell their Chevrolet Lumina to the stepdaughter of a friend who lived down the street, Tiffany Cole. They allowed her to make payments on the car to help her out and she agreed, often driving down to Jacksonville with friends to make those payments. Tiffany and the Sumners became friends and Tiffany would often spend the night at their house when she and her friends went down south. A pleasant girl on the outside, the Sumners had no idea what Tiffany could really be like.

Tiffany Ann Cole was born on December 3, 1981, to her sixteen-year-old mother, Shirley Duncan. Her biological father was in jail. She had no male role model to look up to or who could offer her protection the way a father should. Her mother had a boyfriend, but he was beyond cruel and especially loved to torment Tiffany. At one point, she had a puppy which her stepdad threw against a wall, breaking its neck right in front of her. He was abusive verbally as well as physically and Tiffany claims that as a young girl, he began to molest her, beginning around age eight. As a young teenager, she turned to alcohol and drugs to deal with the pain. In high school, Tiffany was a student who participated in cheerleading and played the flute. She was also a girl scout member but eventually the alcohol and drugs took over her life and she quit her programs and dropped out of school. At one point she fell in love with a boy with severe epilepsy, who ended up breaking her heart and since the only example of love from a man came from an abusive stepfather, this breakup reinforced the belief that she should expect to be treated badly and let down by men. She began looking for love in all the wrong places. In May of 2005, during a six-month period of prostitution, Tiffany ran into a man by the name of Michael Jackson. They were drawn to each other right away and began to get high and sleep together.

Michael James Jackson, born May 12, 1982, had a significant criminal history beginning in childhood. Born to a drug-addicted mother, he was mostly raised by his grandmother. He had multiple felony convictions but only for things like fraud and theft. After meeting Tiffany and becoming close, they took a road trip, first going to Myrtle Beach, then driving to Jacksonville, Florida, where they would be staying with Michael's best friend, Alan Wade. Born May 22, 1987, Alan and Michael had known each other for just over a year. When Tiffany and Michael arrived in Florida, they stayed at Alan's mom's house. After just a few days, though, she kicked them out because she was tired of the loud noises and constant partying. With nowhere else to go and with all their money spent on the nights of drinking and partying, Tiffany remembered that the Sumners lived nearby. The three friends showed up at their doorstep and explained what had happened. The couple was very happy to see Tiffany and invited her and her friends to stay the night. While they were chatting and catching up, Carol mentioned how worried they had been about their house in North Carolina not selling. There was no need to worry, however, because not only did their property sell, but they had also made a $99,000 profit. It was this general statement to a long-time neighbor that sealed the Sumner's fate.

It's difficult to know just whose idea it was to rob the Sumner's. Some say it was both Tiffany and Michael, while others say it was Michael who was the plan maker and master manipulator. Either way, a plan was hatched to rob and kill the loving couple. At some point in June, Alan had contacted his friend, Bruce Nixon Jr., and told him of a plan to rob someone. No other details were given. Then on July 6th, Alan called Bruce, born May 9th, 1987, and asked him if he would be interested in joining the others in digging a hole. Bruce agreed and stole four shovels from his neighborhood. The other three friends drove to Bruce's house in a rented Mazda RX-8 that Tiffany had rented in South Carolina. The group drove around hoping to find a perfectly remote place for the hole to be dug. Alan asked Bruce if he knew of any good places to which Bruce responded that he did. He took them into Georgia, to a wooded area just over the state line. Leaving the car parked on the road, the group walked through the wooded area into a clearing where they began to dig a hole while Tiffany held a flashlight. It was approximately four feet deep and six feet square. Upon completion of the hole, they left the shovels and went back to the car. It was here that Alan asked Michael if Bruce could join in on their robbery plan. Michael agreed. The foursome drove back to Alan's house but his mother would not allow Michael in as she believed him to be a bad influence on her son. Over the next couple of days, it was

Tiffany's job to remain in contact with Carol and Reggie in order to gain information from them about their plans and whereabouts. The foursome also secretly watched the house in order to figure out the Sumner's routine. It was unclear yet as to whether or not the group would enter the home while the couple was gone or if they would simply go in with the couple there. It was ultimately decided that they would enter the home while the couple was there so that they could get their financial information and the means to access their accounts. Michael said that he would kill the victims by injecting them with a lethal dose of their medications. He then promised that the four friends would split the money they received from the Sumner's accounts, each receiving about $50,000. They began making preparations for their plan. Just after midnight on July 8th, 2005, Michael, Tiffany, and Alan went to Wal-Mart and purchased disposable rubber gloves. On the evening of the murders, they went to an Office Depot, where Tiffany bought duct tape and a large roll of plastic wrap. Last, they bought a toy gun that shot plastic pellets.

Around 10pm., on July 8th, 2005, Tiffany drove the other three group members to the Sumner's house in the Mazda. Herself and Michael remained in the car while Alan and Bruce went up to the door. They had the duct tape and toy gun and both were wearing the plastic gloves. After Carol answered the door, Bruce and Alan told her that they were having car trouble and asked if they could use their phone. Carol said of course they could and invited them in. As soon as the boys entered the home, Alan pulled the phone cord out of the wall. Bruce pointed the gun at the couple. Alan grabbed Reggie around the neck and pushed him down into a chair. They told the couple that they wanted credit and debit cards and any other financial information. Carol began pleading with the boys not to hurt them. Bruce took the couple into a spare bedroom where he used duct tape to bind their legs and hands and to cover their mouths and eyes. Alan sent a text message to Michael, informing him that everything was under control. Michael then also entered the home and he and Alan began searching for financial information. They saw a pile of mail and financial statements which they put into a plastic bag. They spotted Reggie's prized coin collection and took that too. Michael told the other two to take the couple into the garage at which point they put them into the trunk of the Lincoln Town car. Tiffany went into the house and grabbed some of their belongings, put them into a bag and took the bag with her to the Mazda. Following the plan, both cars headed towards the gravesite, stopping only once to put gas in the Lincoln. Upon arrival at the site, Michael opened the trunk and apparently began screaming when he saw that the duct tape had become loose and the couple had worked the tape off. It had been over 100 degrees in the trunk. Sweat had caused the tape to loosen. They had also taken the tape off their eyes and were huddled together. Michael ordered Bruce to tape them up again, which he did. Alan then attempted to back up the car to the edge of the grave but, unable to do so, Bruce took over. Michael then sent Bruce up the road to wait with Tiffany at the Mazda. While still alive, the Sumners were taken out of the trunk and pushed into the hole. It is unclear as to who actually did the burying because Alan and Michael each blamed the other. Somehow, Michael ended up getting the personal identification number of the Sumner's bank account. Reports differ on whether he obtained this information from somewhere in the house or if Carol told him the number while being threatened to be buried alive. According to one documentary, Carol had gotten the tape off her mouth again when in the hole. Michael was telling them that if they didn't give up their PIN, they would die, at which point Carol yelled it out. It didn't seem to matter either way though because they continued to shovel dirt onto the scared couple.

After filling the hole, Alan and Michael put the shovels back into the trunk of the Lincoln and drove it up the road to where Tiffany and Bruce were waiting with the Mazda. The four of them drove to

Sanderson, Florida, where they abandoned the Lincoln after wiping it clean of fingerprints. They then drove back to Jacksonville where they immediately went to an ATM and withdrew money from the Sumner's account, before retiring to a hotel. Alan and Tiffany went to another Wal-Mart where they purchased more latex gloves as well as bleach. They returned to the Sumner's home in order to clean up any evidence. They also stole a computer. Bruce stayed with the group for another day and then went home, but Alan remained with Michael and Tiffany who returned to South Carolina, where Tiffany rented two hotel rooms; one for herself and Michael and one for Alan. It should be noted that after returning home, Bruce went to a party with a plastic bag filled with different medications. At one point he announced that he had found a new job murdering people. He stated that he had buried people alive and killed them without mentioning the involvement of anyone else.

On the morning of July 10th, Carol's daughter, Rhonda, decided to report to police the fact that she hadn't been able to get hold of her mother for a few days. Since they kept in touch on a regular basis and spoke every couple days, it was highly unusual for her mother to not return her calls. The next day, the Jacksonville Sheriff's Office (JSO) went to the Sumner's home. The back door of the house was unlocked and in the kitchen there dirty after-dinner plates, which was also highly unusual for the couple. The JSO began to investigate the financial accounts of the couple and they found that large amounts of money had been withdrawn within a short time frame. Video footage from the ATM machines that the group had used showed Michael's face and the silver Mazda in the background. On July 12th, after Rhonda made a plea on local TV networks for the safe return of her parents, the Sheriff's office received a phone call from someone posing as Reggie Sumner. Dispatch contacted Detective David Meacham of the Sheriff's office and put the caller through.

Meacham: Where are you at?

Michael: We're in Delaware right now

Meacham: And what city is that in?

Michael: It's in Corpus

Meacham: Corpus, Delaware?

Michael: Yes

However, the town of Corpus, Delaware does not exist. Next, Tiffany came on the phone posing as Carol.

Meacham: Is this Carol?

Tiffany: Yes, sir, it is.

Meacham: Okay. This is Detective Meacham from the Sheriff's office. How are you doing tonight?

Tiffany: I was sleeping

Meacham: I understand. I understand you have some health problems

Tiffany: Mmhmm

Meacham: Okay. Any other problems?

Tiffany: I'm really tired right now

Meacham: What kind of problems do you have?

Tiffany: Cancer

Meacham: Cancer?

Tiffany: Mmhmm

The detective called Rhonda into the station so that she could listen to the taped conversation. She confirmed that the people posing as the Sumners were definitely not Carol and Reggie. The main reason for the call was to ensure everyone that the Sumners were alive and well and because the bank accounts had been frozen. They asked the detectives to reinstate the accounts, which they did so that they could track the money in order to locate the perpetrators. They also had the phone number from which Michael had called. Using this information, they were able to find that the phone was registered to Michael and that a call had been placed to a car rental agency in Charleston. They also learned that the cell had been used near the Sumner's home the night of the murders. Detective Meacham contacted the rental company and was told that the car had been rented to a Tiffany Cole and that it was overdue. Using the rental car's GPS system, they were able to find that the car had also been near the Sumner's residence during the time of the abduction. Using the cell phone trace, the car's GPS and the photos of Michael at different ATMs, police were able to locate the general whereabouts of the three murderers. On July 14th, with help from Tiffany's brother, who was on probation and threatened with jail, police raided a Best Western hotel in Charleston and arrested Tiffany Cole, Alan Wade, and Michael Jackson. Bruce Nixon was also picked up at his home in Florida.

While Tiffany, Michael, and Alan refused to cooperate with law enforcement, Bruce appeared to have some semblance of a conscience because he broke down and admitted to the crimes right away. He also agreed to lead police to the burial site. For the first time in TV history, documentary footage showed Bruce and detectives at the grave site where Bruce broke down in sobs. Excavation of the site began the next day. The victims were found fully clothed in a crouching position. Reggie had somehow broken his tape and was holding Carol's hand. There was two feet of dirt over their heads. With ten years of homicide under his belt, Detective Meacham said it was one of the saddest and most horrible things he had ever seen. The medical examiner determined that both Reggie and Carol were alive in the hole before they were buried. Their nostrils, mouths, throats, esophagi, and trachea had fine sprays of dirt in them, which indicated that they had inhaled it. They died from mechanical asphyxiation and smothering, caused by the dirt covering their heads while compressing their chests. She said it was the worst case of asphyxiation she'd ever seen. It was "horrendous."

At some point while in jail, but unaware that Bruce had come clean, Michael's grandmother called him.

Grandma: Michael, listen to me and don't say a word. You're in the newspaper. All over the newspaper yesterday and today

Michael: For what?

Grandma: Murder

Michael: What?!

Grandma: Murder. 'Bodies ID'd as former South Carolina couple James and Carol Sumner. Bail was denied for 18-year-old Bruce Nixon of Florida who was arrested and charged with murder, home invasion, robbery, and kidnapping.' He took them to the grave site and everything

Michael: Oh my God. Are you kidding me?

Grandma: It's right here in today's paper

Michael: Bruce took them to the f*****g spot. The f****r showed them where the spot was at?

Grandma: Yes, dear

Michael: *starts panting* Bruce just killed us all

Bruce Nixon told detectives everything that had happened and agreed to testify on behalf of the prosecution. He wasn't sentenced until after he testified against the other three group members, but in the end, he received 45 years for each victim, currently being served concurrently at Century Correctional Institution in Florida. Alan Wade was tried first.

Michael Jackson was the first to be tried. Testifying on his own behalf, Michael stated that the plan was only to rob the Sumners and that it was not going to involve murder. He said that Alan and Bruce went into the house and when they came out they drove off in the Lincoln which he then followed. He claims he had no idea that Reggie and Carol were in the trunk. According to Michael, when they arrived at the hole in Georgia, it was Alan and Bruce who told him where to park and to bring them a flashlight. It was when he arrived at the burial site that he heard Carol moan. He then stated that he questioned what the other two were doing before returning to the Mazda to wait. He did admit to impersonating Reggie. Bruce testified that Michael had been the ringleader and was the one who orchestrated everything.

After stepping down from the witness stand, Carol's daughter, Rhonda, said of Bruce, "I just wanted to hug him. He is a murderer, but in the end, he did the right thing." It was that testimony that she believed sealed Michael's fate because he was found guilty of first degree murder, robbery, and kid-napping, and sentenced to death for each murder. He is currently on death row in Florida.

Alan was next to be tried. Two witnesses who were not identified gave victim impact statements during the penalty phase. Alan's lawyer then called six of their own witnesses to testify including Bruce Nixon, Alan's mom and sister, the mother of a friend, his middle school principal, and his youth pastor. Overall, the witnesses testified that Alan's parents divorced when he was eight and his father disappeared from his life. His mother took him to church regularly and as a kid, he was kind, smart, and well-behaved. After the divorce, his mother was unable to spend a lot of time with him because she had to work a lot to support them. When he was in his teens, his mother had a bout with breast cancer. By his early teens, he began to use drugs. In the sixth grade, he was involuntarily committed to a 72-hour hold because of a drug related incident. When he was sixteen, his mom had to take him out of school or be arrested for his truancy. The next year, his mother kicked him out of the house in an attempt at tough love because his drug use was becoming worse. In 2004 Alan introduced her to Michael, whom she immediately saw as a bad influence on him. Since his arrest and before his trial, Alan had apparently become a model prisoner, obtained his G.E.D and tutored other inmates in math. Nothing seemed to sway the jury, however, because he was found guilty on all counts and voted eleven-to-one to receive the death penalty. He is also currently on death row in Florida.

Tiffany was the last to be tried. Her lawyer argued that she wasn't a major participant in the crimes. He said that she was under the control of her boyfriend Michael, and that he was the mastermind. Tiffany claimed that she believed the crime would only constitute a simple theft and that she didn't knowingly participate in the robberies, kidnapping or murders. She insisted that she did not know that Reggie and Carol were in the trunk of the Lincoln until they arrived at the burial site. The circuit judge, Michael Weatherby did not see it that way, stating that it was she who held the flashlight during the digging of the grave and was there when they were bound and placed in the trunk. He also noted that she was the one who purchased the duct tape and gloves and later pawned the jewelry and computer they had stolen. "She was thoroughly involved," Weatherby stated. "She knew exactly what she was doing and participated without hesitation." It was noted as well that she was the only one of the four who had previously known the Sumners. During the penalty phase, the prosecution called two of the victim's family members who gave impact statements. The defense attorney then called up witnesses who testified that Tiffany was of good character. Three of those witnesses were correctional officers who stated that Tiffany had been no trouble in jail and did not cause any problems. A psychiatrist, Dr. Earnest Miller, testified that she suffered from poly-substance and alcohol abuse, chronic depression, and a personality disorder. He also stated that she had witnessed abuse to family members and had been sexually abused herself by her stepfather. On the other hand, he testified that Tiffany was competent and thus he could not support a plea of insanity. Finally, he stated that she knew right from wrong and had a high average IQ. In the end, Tiffany was also found guilty of all charges and sentenced to death by a 9-3 vote. Upon hearing her fate, she bowed her head and turned to her mother, mouthing the words "I love you". Her lawyer, Quentin Till, said she had been ready for the decision. He visited her in jail that week. "I told her to be strong," he said. "...I still see her being utilized and manipulated by Michael Jackson." Revis Sumner, Reggie's brother, said that Tiffany has since written to the family, asking for forgiveness. He says he has forgiven her, but that doesn't mean she shouldn't suffer for her actions. The Reverend Jean Clark, Reggie's sister has said, "I pray for Tiffany.

I pray for all of them. I'm grieved that these four young people have wasted their lives." Chief Assistant State Attorney, Jay Plotkin, who tried all four cases said, "All of these defendants got exactly what they deserved. Justice was done." After the sentences were given and the trials were over, Reggie's son, Frederick Hallock, said, "You expect some sort of closure or some sort of good feeling when the verdict is read, but it didn't seem to help much. I just know they didn't deserve this." Currently, Tiffany is one of only five women on Florida's death row. At the time of her sentence, she was the sole woman there.

Tiffany, Michael, and Alan all filed appeals after their trials, citing multiple issues. All three were denied and their sentences were upheld. Recently, in 2015, Tiffany filed another appeal, asking for a new trial. She claims that her defense lawyers were ineffective and that she should not have been convicted of first-degree murder since she did not actually bury the bodies herself. But according to Florida law, it doesn't matter who actually committed the murder. Just knowing that it was going to happen is enough to warrant a guilty verdict. At her original trial Tiffany said, "But please remember I didn't do this. I am not the monster that created this, but I regret meeting him," referring to Michael. Upon hearing that Tiffany was asking for a new trial, Reggie's sister, Jean had this to say: "Most people are going to try to come back with something like that after the fact, because they're going to try to find a loophole and get off. But justice has a voice, and justice has to be served." And the thought of going through another trial breaks her heart. "I have family members that are still not the same and never will be the same. In fact, I don't like to involve them too much into things like this, because they can't deal with it."

In 2014, Alan Wade also filed an appeal for a new trial, citing that his lawyers did not do a good job of representing him. His appellate lawyers said that his original defense lawyers barely met with him before the trial and didn't interview witnesses prior to putting them on the stand. They also cited the lack of objections to supposedly questionable evidence. In December 2014, it was decided by the Supreme Court of Florida that his conviction be upheld.

Previous to that, Michael Jackson filed an appeal for a new trial, stating that his lawyers were also ineffective. As with Alan's trial, Michael claims that his lawyers did not make objections to certain evidence when there was clearly an objection to be made. The judge did allow an appeal hearing for his concerns and at the close of the hearing, Michael was allowed to make a statement. It went as follows:

First, I'd like to say that I am guilty of the crimes of first-degree murder, kidnapping, and robbery against Mr. and Mrs. Sumner. My reason for wanting to address the Court today is because of the many lies I told to everyone years ago at pretrial and then trial. I downplayed my involvement to look as if I were not guilty but the truth is that—the truth is that it was my idea to do this. Truly, I did not make anyone do anything. All were willing participants but I was, in fact, the leader. It was my idea to do it. I lied to this Court all throughout my trial testimony, same to [defense counsel and the State]. Even more so I lied to the people who deserve the truth the most, the family of Mr. and Mrs. Sumner, and for that, I am deeply sorry. There are no words that I could ever offer that would convey the depth of my remorse or sorrow, but again I say that I am truly sorry for what I have done and though I'm undeserving, I do ask forgiveness. My desire today is to reconcile the truth to the family of Mr. and Mrs. Sumner and to Your Honor, the attorneys and to the Court record. If necessary, I will answer any and all questions fully and truthfully. Thank you.

His conviction was upheld. Tiffany, Michael, Alan, and Bruce remain in jail today, with the former three on death row.

"It's sad," said Rhonda Alford about her parents. "It took them so long to find each other." Carol and Reggie's ashes sit in an urn in Rhonda's home, forever mixed and blended together.

HUSBAND KILLER : THE TRUE STORY OF AUDREY MARIE HILLEY

ANNA DELANEY

Audrey Marie Hilley

"That woman was pitiful," said Janice Hinds, 50, one of two neighbours who called police and cared for Hilley after spotting her sprawled on the deck of Thomason's home.

"We didn't know she was Marie Hilley. She didn't look like Marie Hilley," said Hinds, who grew up in the same Blue Mountain cotton-mill town as Hilley. "Marie Hilley was a sophisticated lady. She had pride in her looks, her dress."[1]

Her Early Life

Audrey Marie Hilley was born on June 4th, 1933 in Blue Mountain, Alabama. Her parents, Huey and Lucille Frazier, worked hard at the Linen Mill to provide for their family, and Marie (as she was known) was often looked after by relatives when her mother returned to work shortly after she was born.

Huey and Lucille loved their only child but showed their love with material things rather than affection and time. She was always well-dressed and had nice things, and as a result, Marie became rather spoilt. She was well known for her temper tantrums when things didn't go her way, and her parents, possibly out of guilt for not being there, rarely checked her for her behaviour.[2]

The Fraziers were proud people and were determined that their only child would not spend her life working in the same mills as they, and most of the town's inhabitants, had always done. They wanted more for their daughter and instilled in her an ambition to be a secretary, a lofty ambition for someone from a mill town.

In 1945, the Fraziers moved from Blue Mountain to Anniston, and Marie enrolled at Quintard Junior High School. Anniston was a whole new world to the girl who had felt she was above the rest in her old hometown. Marie went from being a big fish in a small pond to a small fish in a much more upscale lake, and for the first time in her life found herself at a disadvantage. In Anniston, all the girls wore nice dresses and what was more, some of their parents were the owners of the same mills that Marie's parents worked at.

Marie threw herself into her studies, making a name for herself as a diligent, intelligent student, and she integrated herself into new social circles – her friends were from privileged families and Marie wanted to be a part of that.

It wasn't just the teachers for whom Marie stood out, though. She was also a pretty girl and had her fair share of the attention from the boys, too. In fact, by the end of the 7th grade of Junior High School, Marie Hilley had been voted the prettiest girl in school by the yearbook staff.

It was around this time that 16-year-old Frank Hilley noticed 12-year-old Marie, and by the time he graduated High School, he was in love.[3]

Frank and Marie

In contrast to the Frazier family, who loved their daughter but showed no affection, Frank Hilley's family was warm and affectionate. The Hilleys worked in the other big industry of the area – pipe making - and even though they did not have much money, Clarence and Carrie Hilley made a happy, comfortable home for their three children – Frank, Jewel and Freeda.

Marie's parents did not approve of Frank – he was not from one of the affluent families of Anniston and Huey and Lucille wanted more for their daughter – but Marie was happy to be Frank's girl, and in return, he treated her like a princess.

Frank joined the Navy after finishing High School and was assigned to Guam but the distance between them bothered Frank. He was worried that with him so far away, and with so much time apart, Marie might find someone else so, on May 8th, 1951, before 17-year-old Marie had even finished High School, the young couple married.

Married Life

Marie remained in Anniston to finish her education and then joined Frank in Long Beach, California before the couple moved to Boston where Frank finished his stint in the Navy. It was while they were in Boston that they discovered Marie was pregnant with their first child, and the couple moved back to Anniston and bought a small home. Frank secured a job with a local foundry, and Marie found work as a secretary. Like all couples, the pair had their ups and downs, but for the most part, they seemed happy.

Their first child, Michael Hilley, was born on November 11th, 1952.

The Troubles Begin

Marie had been brought up to want the best of everything. While Frank was still in the Navy he had sent all of his paychecks home to his young wife, and yet when the time had come for her to join her new husband in California she had no money to pay for the journey. She had been spending his wages without telling him, and his parents had had to finance Marie's travel in order for her to join her new husband.

Despite the extra financial burdens having a young baby places on a family, Marie's spending didn't decrease. She wanted nice clothes and expensive home furnishings, and Frank, not liking to upset his wife, gave in to her, just as her parents had when she was a girl. Marie was a woman who was used to getting her own way.[4]

In 1959 Marie's behaviour began to become more sinister. She started taunting Frank, waving love letters she said were from other men in front of him but not letting him read them. She would then leave the torn up pieces where her husband could find them. Frank pieced them together, and it became clear that his wife had written them herself. When he confronted her she said she was afraid he didn't love her anymore and wanted to make him jealous.

By this time, Marie was spending double her take-home pay from her own job on fine clothes and luxuries. To prevent Frank, who was extremely responsible financially, from finding out she would get up early in the morning to check the mail and hide the bills.

Marie became pregnant again, and on January 14th, 1960 she gave birth to a baby daughter, whom they named Carol Marie.[5]

Carol

By the time Carol was born, things should have been looking up for the family. Frank had been promoted at work, and Marie had developed a reputation as a first class executive secretary. However, as the family's income rose, so did Marie's spending. Furthermore, she was becoming known for a peculiar situation at work. While her bosses loved her for her politeness and diligence, her co-workers greatly disliked her. They found her to be very judgemental of those around her and felt that she put on airs and graces and acted as if her co-workers were 'beneath' her. When she became disliked she would leave, and complain to friends and family that her colleagues had 'ganged up' on her and driven her from her job. Her employers, though, always gave her exemplary references, and she never found it difficult to get another job. In fact, Marie Hilley worked for some of the most powerful and affluent men in Anniston.[6]

Marie was disappointed with her daughter, Carol. She wanted her daughter to wear pretty dresses and have bows in her hair, while Carol was more of a tomboy and would often go to football games with her father. The pair developed a close father/daughter relationship and Marie was deeply resentful and jealous. She lamented the fact that her daughter was not feminine and demure and the pair argued constantly. Marie was much closer to her son, Mike, and like her parents before her never dished out discipline. Materially, the children wanted for nothing. Emotionally, it was a different story.

Going Up in the World

In 1962, Marie instigated a move to McClellan Boulevard, which was much closer to the houses of the affluent residents of Anniston that she so desperately tried to emulate. She felt that they were 'her' people. That same year, Marie's parents – Huey and Lucille moved in with the Hilleys.[7]

Marie's behaviour was becoming more and more out of control, and Frank was becoming increasingly concerned. He would often sit up with her during the night as she shook violently, unable to calm her. Perhaps the financial hole she had dug for the family was beginning to take its toll on Marie's psyche – by this time she had opened a Post Office Box and was having some of her bills sent there in order to avoid detection by Frank.

When the money ran out Marie started taking out loans. Frank was a well-respected man in the area and loans were secured against his good name and standing in the community. But creditors became concerned when bills and loan payment dates came and went without being settled, as Frank had always been a man who paid on time.[8]

On December 11th, 1965, Marie's father, Huey, died of cancer at the age of 57.[9]

In 1972, Mike graduated from High School and decided to pursue a career in the ministry, for which he went away to college.

Marie's behaviour towards her daughter, Carol, became more extreme. She often accused her of being a lesbian and would rant at Carol's female friends. Her paranoia at being found out in the lies regarding money must have been affecting her, because she also, around this time, stopped Frank from talking to his friends on the 'phone. It was also around this period of time that Frank Hilley became sick.[10]

Frank

During 1974 Frank had long periods of sickness. He put his frequent illnesses down to something he'd eaten, but soon the fatigue, vomiting and nausea could not be explained away by food. One day Frank came home from work early after succumbing to yet another bout of sickness, to find his wife in bed with her boss. His wife's spending suddenly made sense – she was sleeping with her employers for money. Frank was disgusted with his wife's behaviour but felt too ill and weak to deal with it. Instead, he turned to his son, Mike, who was by this time an ordained minister.[11]

However, that phone call, in which Frank arranged to meet Mike in Georgia where he now lived, was overheard by Audrey, who was listening in on an extension. From that moment on, Frank's symptoms worsened considerably, and he became seriously ill.[12]

On May 19th, 1975 Frank couldn't stand it any longer, and he consulted Dr Earl Jones, who diagnosed him initially with a viral stomach ache.[13] Dr Earl prescribed various medications, but nothing seemed to be helping. Frank's sister Freeda came to visit him, and he told her that he feared he was going to die, as he had never been so sick. He also told her that Marie had been administering him medicine via a syringe on the Dr's orders.[14]

On May 23rd, 1975, Frank was admitted to the Regional Medical Center. Tests indicated liver failure, and subsequently infectious hepatitis.[15] Frank was desperately ill, jaundiced and hallucinating. Mike, who had travelled to be with his father, had to restrain Frank from jumping out of the window. In the early hours of May 25th, Mike left the hospital to pick up his Grandmothers so that they could see Frank, but when he returned his mother was asleep and his father was dead. Frank Hilley was 45.[16]

Because of Frank's sudden death, an autopsy was performed, with Marie's blessing. Tests showed that Frank did indeed have hepatitis, along with swelling of the lungs and kidneys, inflammation of the stomach, and bilateral pneumonia.[17]

Life After Frank

With Frank's death being confirmed as being of natural causes, Marie made a claim on his life insurance and received a payment of

$31,140.[18] Marie went on a spending spree, indulging her love of luxury items. She bought new clothes, jewelery, and a new car. Her mother, Lucille, was still living with Marie and Carol and received a diamond ring. Carol herself was treated to numerous gifts, including a car and a stereo. It was hardly the behaviour of a grieving widow.[19]

In 1976 Mike and his then wife Teri moved in with the family. Shortly after Frank's death, Lucille had been diagnosed with cancer. Her health was failing and they were happy to help. However, it wasn't a good move for the young couple. Marie was restless, and often complained to anyone who would listen that nobody loved her, and would frequently complain about her boss and her job. She was highly dissatisfied with her life, and to make matters worse Marie and Carol fought endlessly, making family life fraught. Mike would often find himself torn between his mother, who would constantly demand his attention, and his wife, Teri, who had begun experiencing ill health since moving in with Marie. Hospitalised four times with illness, Teri also suffered a miscarriage, and the young couple decided to move out.

They found an apartment and were ready to move in, but the night before their move Marie's house caught fire. Mike and Teri moved into their apartment, with Marie, Carol and Lucille in tow. Repairs were soon made to Marie's house, but the night before his mother was due to go home, Mike's neighbour's apartment suffered the same fate and went up in flames. Mike and Teri had no choice but to move back in with Marie, Carol and Lucille. They were back where they began.[20]

A Strange Series of Events

Mike and Teri finally found their own home and moved away from Marie. On January 4th, 1977, Lucille lost her battle against widespread, aggressive cancer. Marie again came into money – a small sum of $600 from a burial policy.

Marie became well known to the local police. She was constantly reporting strange occurrences at her home. As well as petty thefts, she claimed that a fire had been started in her closet late one night. Coincidentally, Marie's neighbour, Doris Ford reported an almost identical fire in her own house (to which Marie had a key) the same night. There followed a succession of reports by both women of nuisance phone calls and other grievances.

Marie came up with many theories about where the harassment of both herself and her neighbour was coming from. She told Detective Gary Caroll that she suspected someone at the phone company of making the calls, as the calls seemed only to happen when the trace was taken off of her phone. She also claimed that one of her former employers had tried to force her to have sex and was harassing her because of her refusal. Yet another theory put forward by Marie was that, shortly after Frank's death, two men had arrived at her house demanding repayment of gambling debts.

When police put a trace on Doris Ford's phone, however, the calls were traced back to the Jenkins Manufacturing Plant, which just so happened to be where Marie was working.[21]

In 1978, Marie and Carol moved to Florida to live with Mike and Teri. Carol had just graduated, and Marie found herself a job in an office. Her out of control spending habits continued to cause problems when she ran up over $600 on Mike's credit card, promising to pay him back. This living arrangement only lasted a few short months, however, before Marie and Carol returned to Anniston.[22]

Mike and Teri were happy to see Marie leave. By that time they had a baby son called Joshua, and Mike feared that Marie would take the baby and disappear as she seemed to have an unhealthy fixation on him.[23]

Carol's Turn

Marie had no home of her own to return to when she and Carol moved back to Anniston. At first, they stayed with Freeda, Frank's sister, and then they moved in with Carrie Hilley, Frank's mother.

Once they were settled at Carrie's house, the strange happenings recommenced. Items went missing, phone lines were cut, and small fires were started. Illness also struck the household – Carrie Hilley started suffering from nausea and vomiting.

Marie started a new job, and very quickly started an affair with her boss, Harold Dillard, and began manipulating him to leave his wife. At the same time, she also started seeing Calvin Robertson, an old school friend. Calvin believed Marie when she told him she had cancer and needed expensive treatment, and he gladly gave her the money for the 'fictitious' illness. When Marie told him some time later that she was now cancer-free he was elated, and so smitten that he would have done anything for her.

It was also during this time that Marie began buying insurance policies. Not only did she take out fire insurance, cancer insurance, and her own life insurance, she also took out insurance policies on the lives of her two children. Mike was insured for $25,000 while Carol had two policies on her life, totalling $39,000.

Carol's senior prom came in April 1979. During the evening Carol started to feel ill. It wasn't enough to make her leave the party, though, so she ignored her symptoms. The next day, however, she was so ill during a church service that she had to leave the service early and vomited in the car park. Coincidentally, Carrie Hilley had also taken ill at church and was taken to hospital after fainting.[24]

By August 1979 Carol had been admitted to the Emergency Room several times with nausea and vomiting. After yet another episode of sickness in August, Marie gave her daughter an injection into her hip, which she said would ease the nausea. Instead of easing, however, Carol's illness took a serious downturn. Not only did the injection not ease Carol's sickness, it also caused her fingers and legs to become numb and weak.

On August 22nd, 1979 she was admitted to the Anniston Hospital by Dr Warren Sarrell. When, by August 29th Dr Sarrell had been unable to find a cause for Carol's symptoms, he sent her for a psychiatric evaluation at the Carraway Methodist Hospital in Birmingham. While under the care of Dr John Elmore, Carol was given two further injections by her mother – injections which, she was told, would help with her weak legs. She told Carol that the injections had been supplied by Doris Ford, who was a registered nurse, and that Carol could tell no-one as Doris would get into trouble if she was found out.

On September 18th, 1979, with Carol still in the hospital, Marie asked Dr Elmore what was wrong with her daughter. He told her that she was suffering from vitamin deficiencies and malnutrition, and, in his opinion, lead poisoning. Carol took exception to this diagnosis and, against Dr Elmore's advice, discharged Carol from the hospital.

On September 19th, Carol was once again admitted to the hospital, this time to the University of Alabama Hospital in Birmingham. The same day, Marie was arrested as her fraudulent ways finally caught up with her. Her arrest was what, ultimately, saved Carol's life. Marie was taken in for questioning, and Carol was examined by Dr Brian Thompson, who noticed that, along with the numbness in her hands and feet, Carol also had striations on her nails, called Aldridge Mee's Lines. He explained that these markings were typical of arsenic poisoning, and ordered tests on Carol's hair.

The initial findings revealed that Carol had over 50 times the normal arsenic level of human hair. Shockingly, when more detailed tests were carried out on October 3rd, 1979 they showed that the hair close to Carol's scalp had over 100 times the normal levels, while hair further down the hair shaft the levels were lower, right down to zero at the ends. This indicated, according to Forensic Scientist John Case, that Carol had been systematically poisoned with arsenic over a period of four to eight months, with the dosages given in increasingly higher strengths.

Furthermore, with Marie unable to be with her daughter, Carol's conditioned improved dramatically during her time at the hospital.[25]

On the strength of these findings, Frank Hilley's body was exhumed, and once again large levels of arsenic were found. His cause of death was changed to that of arsenic poisoning. The same substance was also discovered to have been present in both Lucille Frazier and Carrie Hilley (who had died recently) at the time of their deaths, although not fatal amounts.[26]

On October 9th, 1979, while still incarcerated for the fraudulent charges, Marie Hilley was arrested for the attempted murder of Carol. As part of their ongoing, and increasingly serious, investigations the Anniston police found a vial in Marie's purse – a vial which testing confirmed contained arsenic.

On November 9th, 1979, Marie made bail and was released, under the name of Emily Stephens, to a local motel. However, Marie was not going to just sit and await her trial, and somewhere between October 9th and October 18th, Marie disappeared. A note was found in her motel room, suggesting that she 'might' have been kidnapped.

Audrey Marie Hilley was now a fugitive and would remain so for more than three years.[27]

A New Identity

There were only a few clues for the police to go on after Marie disappeared. Margaret Key, Marie's Aunt, reported that her home had been broken into and that her car and some clothes had disappeared. The police called in the FBI, but once the car was found abandoned in Georgia the trail went cold very quickly.

On January 11th, 1980, Marie Hilley, still a fugitive, was indicted for the murder of her husband, Frank Hilley.

Marie, meanwhile, had assumed a new identity in Florida. Robbi Hannon, as she was now known, was working her charm on a man called John Homan. Robbi told John tales of her imaginary tragic past, and John, who hadn't had the easiest of lives himself, fell for both the stories and for Robbi. She told him that she had lost her children in a car accident and John felt as though he had found a kindred spirit.

He fell in love, hook, line, and sinker.

On May 29th, 1981 Robbi and John were married, after which they moved to Marlow, New Hampshire. They both found work there and rented a house. Robbi's new job was in customer service at the Central Screw Corporation, where she excelled. The men found her to be fun, while her co-workers, for the most part, found her pleasant, although a few took a dislike to her. She regaled the staff with stories of a wealthy family in Texas, whose fortune she would inherit one day, and garnered sympathy by telling them about her two children dying in a car accident.

She would also talk of an identical twin sister called Teri Martin, who lived in Texas, making frequent reference to her.

Robbi would, from time to time, complain of searing headaches, and told John that she was seeking treatment from specialists. Until one day, Robbi came to John and told him it had been discovered that she was suffering from an incurable blood disease. It was her twin sister, Teri, who would be looking after Robbi when she made one last trip to Texas in search of a cure, and in September 1982, Robbi left Marlow to seek treatment.

Of course, there was no incurable disease, and no twin sister, either. Robbi only stayed in Texas for a few days, and then made her way to Florida, where she bleached her hair blond, and found work as a secretary, using the name Teri Martin. During her six weeks at her new job, Teri confided in her boss, Jack McKenzie, about her terminally ill twin sister Robbie. In early November, Teri called Jack and told him Robbi had died, and that she was needed in New Hampshire.

On November 10th, 'Teri' called John Homan and told him his wife had died, and the following day she flew back to New Hampshire.

During her time away, 'Teri' had lost a lot of weight, and changed her hair color to blond, so John easily accepted that this was his dead wife's twin sister. The pair went to the local paper and placed an obituary for Robbi, and then John took Teri to his wife's workplace – The Central Screw Corporation – and introduced the workers to Robbi's twin sister. While some of the staff accepted Teri's appearance, some did not and were highly suspicious.

Teri insisted on moving in with John Homan, saying they needed to help each other grieve, and she found herself a job as a secretary at a book printing company.

Meanwhile, the suspicions were still rising at Robbi's old workplace, and a few of the doubters decided to take a closer look into Robbi's obituary. Their suspicions were confirmed when they discovered that the details mentioned in the paper were fictitious, and they took those suspicions to the police.

Arrested

On January 12th, 1983, the police apprehended Teri at work. They had been watching her and thought she might be another fugitive, Terry Lynn Clifton. However, when they asked her her name she told them it was Audrey Marie Hilley, and that she was wanted for fraud. The local police ran a check on her name and discovered that she was wanted for much more than bad checks.

On January 19th, 1983, Marie was brought back to Anniston. Carol was desperate to see her mother, to find some answers, but although Marie professed her love for her daughter she gave no explanation for the poisoning. Prosecutors were worried that Carol's love for her mother would go in Marie's favour and that Carol would not say anything against her mother.

They needn't have worried.

Carol's testimony about her mother giving her the injections was solid. Marie had told her attorneys that after her arrest in 1979 she had been interviewed but she failed to mention that that interview had been recorded. During that interview, Marie admitted to giving Carol the injections and the recording was there for all to hear. Carol's defense fell apart.

The jury needed only three hours to return their verdicts – guilty of the murder of Frank Hilley, and of the attempted murder of Carol Hilley.

Judge Sam Monk sentenced Marie to life imprisonment for Frank's murder, plus twenty years for the poisonings, and on June 9th, 1983, Marie was taken to Tutwiler State Women's Prison in Wetumpka, Alabama.

Marie's Escape

Marie was a perfect prisoner. She never caused trouble and was classified as a minimum security prisoner. This classification meant that she was eligible for leave from the prison. Between late 1986 and February 1987, Marie had left prison for eight hours on four occasions, returning on time with each leave.

On February 19th, 1987, Marie left the prison on a three-day leave pass. John had, by this time, moved to Anniston so that he and his wife could spend her leave together whenever they could.

On February 22nd, Marie arranged to meet John at her parents' graves. Marie never showed up, and John found, instead, a note from his wife.

"I hope you will be able to forgive me," it read. *"I'm getting ready to leave. It will be best for everybody. We'll be together again. Please give me an hour to get out of town."*

John took the note to the police, and, given Marie's past cunning, they assumed she was already far out of state, and started, once again, searching for her.[28]

Her Death

Marie hadn't gone far. On February 26th, 1987, Aniston police received a phone call. Marie had been found huddled behind a house, apparently having wandered in the woods for four days. The weather had been terrible – heavy rain and low temperatures – and Marie was suffering from hypothermia and delirium. Marie started having convulsions, and, in the ambulance on the way to the hospital, Audrey Marie Hilley took her last breath.

On February 28th, 1987, Marie was buried next to her husband, Frank, at their children's request.[29] Her second husband, John Homan, died two years later in 1989 while working as a caretaker in Anniston. He intervened in a fight and was stabbed to death. Marie's note to John, in which she said that they would be together again, had come true a lot sooner than anyone would have predicted.[30]

www.ingramcontent.com/pod-product-compliance
Lightning Source LLC
Chambersburg PA
CBHW051834130726
47987CB00002B/538